HURRY
LESS
WORRY
LESS

for

Moms

More Books by Judy Christie

Hurry Less, Worry Less

Hurry Less, Worry Less at Christmas

Hurry Less, Worry Less at Work

Hurry Less, Worry Less for Families

Goodbye Murphy's Law: Whatever Can Go Wrong,
God Can Make Right

Awesome Altars (coauthored with Mary Dark)

Fiction

Gone to Green

Goodness Gracious Green

The Glory of Green

Rally 'Round Green

JUDY CHRISTIE

HURRY LESS WORRY LESS

for Moms

Abingdon Press
Nashville

HURRY LESS, WORRY LESS
for Moms

This book is printed on acid-free paper.

Library of Congress Cataloging-in-Publication Data

Christie, Judy Pace, 1956–
 Hurry less, worry less for moms / Judy Christie.
  p. cm.
 ISBN 978-0-687-65915-9 (book - pbk./trade pbk. : alk. paper)
1. Mothers—Religious life. 2. Time management—Religious
aspects—Christianity. 3. Peace of mind—Religious
aspects—Christianity. I. Title.
 BV4529.18.C47 2011
 248.8'431--dc23

                                                                2011032152

All scripture quotations, unless otherwise indicated, are taken from the Holy Bible, New International Version®, NIV®. Copyright © 1973, 1978, 1984, 2011 by Biblica, Inc.™ Used by permission of Zondervan. All rights reserved worldwide. www.zondervan.com.

The "NIV" and "New International Version" are trademarks registered in the United States Patent and Trademark Office by Biblica, Inc.™

Scripture quotations noted CEB are from the Common English Bible. Copyright © 2011 by the Common English Bible. All rights reserved. Used by permission. www.CommonEnglishBible.com.

Scripture marked NRSV is from the New Revised Standard Version of the Bible, copyright 1989, Division of Christian Education of the National Council of the Churches of Christ in the United States of America. Used by permission. All rights reserved.

Scripture quotations from *THE MESSAGE*. Copyright © by Eugene H. Peterson 1993, 1994, 1995, 1996, 2000, 2001, 2002. Used by permission of NavPress Publishing Group.

Scripture marked KJV is from the King James or Authorized Version of the Bible.

11 12 13 14 15 16 17 18 19 20—10 9 8 7 6 5 4 3 2 1

MANUFACTURED IN THE UNITED STATES OF AMERICA

To my sisters-in-law, encouragers for many years:

Jane, Cindy, Isabelle, and Mary Frances

Contents

With Gratitude

I owe so much to the many moms who took time from their busy lives to offer wisdom and guidance for this book, and to friends and family members who encourage me on each project. Deep thanks go to: Africa, Annette, Barbara McG., Becky C., Beth B., Bonnie, Brenda, Carol G., Carol L., Diana, Elizabeth H., Ella, Gaye, Ginger, Jane A., Janel, Jill, Kacee, Kara, Kathie, Kathleen, Karen E., Karen R., Karen S., Kate, Kerri, Laura K., Laura N., Mary Ann E., Mary Frances, Mary T., Mer, Monica, Nancy, Peggy, Sarah B., Sukie, Susan Y., Susy E., Suzanne, and Yvonne.

My love and special thanks go to my Grace Community United Methodist Church family, including Pastor Rob Weber and Barbara Montgomery, who helped so much with recent Hurry Less, Worry Less books. Warm gratitude goes to the children of Lurain Grounds, for sharing their mother with me for so many years and offering memories upon her death; to the late Alisa Stingley, for editing and offering a listening ear; Pat Lingenfelter, friend and super cheerleader rolled into one; and Etta Wilson and Janet Grant, agents, mentors, and friends.

Always, thanks to my husband, Paul, who doesn't hurry and doesn't worry—and helps me every day with everything I do.

Finally, my eternal thanks for the memory of my mother, who was, quite simply, wonderful.

Introduction

Ultimately, the work you do in raising your children is the Lord's work because they are a gift from God, entrusted to us for a period of time. —A Mom's Thoughts

As a young working mother, a college friend found herself with an important meeting on her schedule—and no babysitter. With briefcase and diaper bag, she set out, power suit adjusted, child in arms.

Proud of herself for making the many pieces of her life fit, she marched into the client's office, a smile on her face and paperwork ready. Her infant son chose that moment to dirty his diaper in an act of epic proportions.

To hear my friend tell it, the meeting pretty much fell apart after that.

A recent chat with a young mom brought to light a challenge of a different variety. Her children were invited to a party that evening and were supposed to dress as pirates. She had nothing for their costumes. Couldn't even think of anything. Her brain had apparently locked up somewhere between getting the children to school, getting herself to work, and getting pirate costumes assembled.

Introduction

A colleague scoots out of work each afternoon to pick up her daughter and drop her at an after-school program. The friend makes up the work time at home on her computer late at night.

Then there was this recent note from a mom after a tough day: "My brain feels like it is about to explode. Or implode. Or just 'plode."

Welcome to the challenging, creative world of hurried and worried moms—a remarkable group of people who are so different in many ways, and so alike in love for family and busyness of schedules.

In my life and work, I visit with thousands of people who are overloaded, overscheduled, stressed out, and worn out.

Moms top this list.

While you don't have to be a mother to be rushed, that precious role brings added layers of responsibility and activity. In writing *Hurry Less, Worry Less at Work*; *Hurry Less, Worry Less for Families*; and *Hurry Less, Worry Less at Christmas*, I realized anew the pressures, challenges, and rewards for moms.

Dear busy moms, this book is for you.

You, moms, juggle and struggle and look for ways to get more done in less time. You are loving and creative, often short on sleep, and long on laundry. Your to-do list could strike fear in the heart of the busiest CEO. You may be eager to enjoy each day more but sometimes don't quite know where to begin.

You know how it can feel. Every time you turn around, someone wants or needs something from you. That doesn't leave much time for stepping back to assess how things are going—and even less for renewal and relaxation.

You probably want to learn to say no more often and simplify your calendar. You want to live by your priorities, spend fun time with your families, and have time here and there for yourself.

You are nothing short of exceptional in all you want and need to do, and in how much you care about being great mothers. You make a difference every single day.

One of the great joys of visiting with mothers is observing how different they are—and yet how strikingly similar. I hear stories from new moms, tender women with brand-new babies who are trying to learn one of the hardest jobs in the world. Then there are the moms of elementary school children and teens, navigating different terrain. There are those who send their children off to school each day, and those who settle around the table to homeschool. Some think about the upcoming empty nest or try to stay on top of their college child's activities. Others prepare for the day their child will go to kindergarten.

Many moms work outside the home—in jobs that range from minimum-wage food services work, such as my beloved mother did, to high-powered executive jobs. Others choose to use their skills as stay-at-home moms and are diligent with family and volunteer work.

Some are single, handling parenting largely on their own, or are moms whose husbands are deployed overseas or must work out of town to make ends meet. Some have adult children and find themselves dealing with complex daily issues or even rearing grandchildren, a new, often unplanned mom job. Blended families are ordinary these days, and stepmoms add their challenges to the list. They want to make sure that they have the right children at the right house at the right time—and that they are loving and supportive. Preparing for this book, I have observed foster moms, who help children with enormous needs, and adoptive moms with thrilling stories of the challenges of adoption and the delight of rearing these children God has brought into their homes.

My own hardworking, loving mama was my early role model in the art of motherhood. Sometimes we overlook how spectacular the influence of moms is—and how tough their routines.

My hope is that this book will help moms replace full schedules with full hearts and will offer tips that work in everyday life. Most moms don't need to be taught, as the old saying goes; they just need to be reminded. Moms often know very well what they need to do, but they're so overwhelmed they can't find time to do it. A reminder can help slow mom down and allow time to take inventory of the parenting life.

The thoughts of everyday moms are woven throughout these pages. Their warm, wise, and witty remarks speak of challenges that range from caring for a sick baby to looking out for an older parent, making hard decisions about where to work and when to work, about setting priorities and sticking with them, about trusting God all along the way.

This book includes practical tools, which serve as reminders that there are no cookie-cutter families. Individual moms have to figure out what works for them. Each chapter offers a "A Mom's Thoughts," practical and inspiring words, and "Mom's Quiet Corner," a section for prayer and reflection, including a tip from a busy mother, a Bible passage recommended by a mom, a mom-to-mom suggestion, and a prayer for the journey as a parent.

Maybe you, moms, have lots of children or only one. Perhaps your children are in diapers—or off to college. Maybe you are settling in to life as a new mom or wondering how to live with teens or to counsel adult children. No matter what season of time a mom is in, she can use these tips to slow down and enjoy each day more.

At the end of *Hurry Less, Worry Less for Moms*, you will find a study guide to be used on your own or with a friend or a group and "reminder" tips to continue to make progress.

Take a deep breath, moms, and decide to make needed changes or to refresh your dreams for your lives. Look forward to the process, and celebrate your victories. You can hurry less and worry less. Even as busy moms!

CHAPTER ONE

A Map for Mom

Being the Person You Are Meant to Be

Encouraging Word: *You can make needed changes.*

Everyday Step: *Set aside a few minutes to assess your life.*

When I worry if I am doing enough or am good enough, I pray about it and know that the only person I am to please is God. I need to ask for direction in my life. If I am doing what God wants, that is enough. I have peace inside when I focus on God and not on my own insecurities.—A Mom's Thoughts

In the sixth grade, I was sent on an errand to a neighborhood store. While I was there, I was unable to resist the urge to linger at each counter, captivated by a host of items that called out to a girl my age.

Engrossed in one display near the wall, I took a step back—and tumbled into a cardboard box sitting behind me in the narrow aisle.

As awkward moves go, this was a doozy. I was now sitting on my bottom in the oversized box, with my legs hanging over the side. The box was too big to hop out of, but too small for me to turn around and stand up. I certainly wasn't going to call for help, letting someone else see my predicament.

My problem-solving skills began to mature in that moment. I rocked the box until I got enough momentum to turn it over. Then I crawled out, looked around to make sure no one had noticed, righted the box, and scampered out as though nothing had happened. I'm not sure I even bought the item I had been sent for.

Perhaps as a mom you know that feeling.

One minute you are standing right where you want to be, and the next you've tumbled into an uncomfortable place. You need a good supply of problem solving.

Everywhere you turn you'll find moms who love their children with all their hearts but who are desperate to slow down and enjoy life more. They make hundreds of great decisions each and every day, taking care of the smallest details and the biggest catastrophes. Even so, they too often feel as though they somehow don't measure up or can't get it quite right.

They run as fast as they can, but remain behind where they think they should be. Trying to close that gap brings on an immense amount of frustration and guilt.

Mom Fuel

Getting out of the box requires step-by-step focus and uses mom fuel you might not even know you have—energy you get from making a fresh appraisal of what you love about being a mom, from strengthening your faith and doing more of what matters most to you.

Perhaps you need to be reminded of how much you accomplish every day, how special you are, and how your gifts and talents make you unique. Maybe you can take a step back and consider what works well in your life and what needs tweaking. Moms are geniuses at getting things done. They cherish their children and want to be present in the moment.

Most moms go at such a rapid clip that they seldom take time to gauge the life they long for. They may know what they need or want to do but can't quite get around to doing it. Or they have it all figured out—and still find themselves slipping back into old patterns that don't work for them and their families.

Have you ever zoomed through a big mall or airport, trying to figure out where you need to go? You rely on one of those maps that says "you are here," but that doesn't automatically get you where you want to be.

So it is for moms.

You are here.

Now's a good time to consider anew where "here" is.

Get your bearings on the map that is your life.

Figure out where you want to go.

That will help you determine how to get there.

And then set out. If you get turned around, step back, regroup, and get back on the right path. You'll probably have to stop and get your bearings again and again. Don't lose heart if it doesn't all go according to that neat little plan you have in your mind or spelled out on your calendar.

You are here, Mom.

Remember: Wherever "here" is in your life, it is a perfect spot from which to take a new look. "Here" is the place where God is going to use you; it is the place where you will grow; it is the spot where you will touch the lives of your family members in a way that no one else on the entire planet can.

"Here" is the jumping-off point for making changes you have needed or wanted to make for a while or for helping you find contentment in the life you have.

You are here, Mom.

And you're not here alone. God guides you and is in control.

Many women share your concerns and joys and empathize with your battles. Words like *organized chaos* and *bombardment* and *typical overloaded family* sprinkle the conversations of mothers. Pause and ask God to help you. Embark on this as a private journey, or invite other moms to travel this road with you. Destination: fuller and richer time with your family.

Most mothers have dreams for themselves and their families. These often include more joy, peace, calm, faith, and fun; more organization and less procrastination; a good nap now and then; and help with the logistics of life. They want to be better at balancing home and work. They want good things for their children. They would like to feel that once, just once, they could complete something.

Take a deep breath. Climb out of your box, and begin to think about what you want your life to look like. Figuring this out may not be the easiest thing to do, but it is fulfilling and can help you find more meaning as a mom.

You, Your Family, and God

Get to know yourself and your family better, being aware of what makes you tick, your strengths, and the areas that may need improvement. Consider your relationship with God. Depend on others.

This is not a do-it-yourself project, although it is intensely personal. You will need the interaction and influence of people around you, from a child to a mate to your best gal pal. You may get out of the box by yourself, but it's tough to stay on the right path without the support of others. Call upon family and friends, a community of faith, and your coworkers.

Perhaps you are like many moms who want to live more fully—more meaningfully, joyfully, peacefully, faithfully, prayerfully, thankfully, hopefully, powerfully. That goal of living fully is within reach and can be adapted to match your life and your family, different from any other person or family in the entire world.

Christ said, "I have come that they may have life, and have it to the full" (John 10:10). That is a promise that moms can lean on every single day.

Your family needs you to live fully. The world needs you to live fully.

And *you* need you to live fully.

As you consider moving toward being the mom you want to be, know that you can do it. This can work for you, in your life. It may mean making changes, some that are so easy they surprise you and some that are so tough they scare you. You may have to teach yourself to live in the moment and not give in to fear about the future.

Why is it important to hurry less and worry less as a mom?

It is impossible to live fully when you are hurried and worried most of the time. Unless you can learn to slow down and fret less, you may never feel satisfied with your daily life, content, or calm. You may spend your days thinking *if only* or *some day*. I have seen this in the lives of many women, including my own. Hurry and worry are roadblocks to getting where you want to be, wherever that is, whoever you are.

Remember the map mentioned above? Imagine your frustration if you followed directions and ran into a brick wall, unable to get to the right destination. So it goes as a harried mom who tries to do too much and is anxious too much of the time.

One of a Kind

As you ponder your life, remember that you and your family are one of a kind. Consider your individual situation as you make choices and shape changes.

You don't have to be supermom. You are called to be a loving mom who does her best.

You don't have to have all the answers. Now and then you just have to ask the right questions.

One of the young mothers I admire greatly is a part-time teacher and the mother of three children. She consistently stresses the importance of being true to yourself and your family: "My main suggestion as a mom is not to compare yourself to others. I've had to realize that I can contribute what I can, but my focus is on my family. We have dinner together virtually every night. My husband and I go out together almost every weekend. Raising balanced, well-adjusted children is key to me, as well as having a good marriage. Both of my parents were married twice. Honestly, before we married, I didn't really know what a good marriage looked like. Therefore, I am not the übervolunteer in the community, church, or school. I do what I can. At another time in my life I will probably go back to teaching full-time and have more time to volunteer. I will enjoy it then, but right now I cannot do that and keep my mind."

A mother of eight avoids "the comparison trap." She says, "I look to God's word to reshape my thinking. I know the Lord has a plan for my life."

Part of this journey is learning to know yourself better, an ongoing adventure. You will grow as you understand who you are and listen for God's guidance in your life.

To help you on this journey:

Depend on God. "Come near to God and he will come near to you" (James 4:8).

Appreciate your calling as a mom. "For we are God's workmanship, created in Christ Jesus to do good works, which God prepared in advance for us to do" (Ephesians 2:10).

Try again when you stumble. "Create in me a pure heart, O God, / and renew a steadfast spirit within me. / Do not cast me from your presence / or take your Holy Spirit from me. / Restore to me the joy of your salvation / and grant me a willing spirit, to sustain me" (Psalm 51:10-12).

Lay those words down against your life, and use them for support. Your role as a mother is a special calling. You will need to renew your spirit from time to time. Don't be afraid, God tells you. No matter what motherhood throws at you, God will be there to guide you, to help when you feel overwhelmed.

Figure out steps to take. *You are here. Where do you want or need to go as a mom?*

Decide what brings meaning to your life as a mom. You may need to learn to say no to activities or commitments that take too much time. You may want to say yes to a daily quiet time or a visit with a friend. You may have taken a detour from spending time with your family and need to find your way back. You may search for ways to be more peaceful and joyful in the midst of an often noisy, cranky world. Maybe you have found yourself slipping into negative thinking or being too grumpy with people you love. You may yearn for fun days with your family or a little more exercise to help you stay fit.

Celebrate your accomplishments as a mom. You're doing a permanent 24/7 job, nothing temporary here. This role comes without a written job description and requires a range of skills including providing medical care, teaching, accounting, cooking, party planning, and even fashion designing. One minute you're trying to pay the bills, and the next you're breaking up a squabble over the TV remote and reminding the children they're supposed to share. Or you're settling into a meeting at work and get a call about a sick child, or settling into bed after a long, hard day and your teen wants to tell you about a problem at school.

The Challenges, the Benefits

Momhood comes with many challenges, but it brings spectacular benefits, including the special love a child has for his or her mom, a relationship unlike any other, laughter, hugs, and stories you'll be telling till the end of your life—plus the impact that you will have on the world through your children.

Dozens of mothers reminded me anew that this is a journey, one that comes with many twists and turns. Your path may well change with seasons of time, depending on the ages of your children or family circumstances. Being a mom is like being on a long-distance run that will be jogged each hour of each day for years to come.

A Fresh Look, a Sacred Calling

Perhaps you are a new mom and want to outline your goals for motherhood. Or maybe you're a mom watching your children get older and looking for ways to enhance your family time. Maybe you're headed back to work after a season away—or taking a break from your career. Whatever stage of motherhood you are in, you can take a new look at your life and ponder the path you want to take.

FIND WHAT WORKS FOR YOU AND HOW YOU CAN BE THE PERSON YOU WERE CALLED TO BE, TO DO YOUR BEST AND DEPEND ON GOD FOR HELP.

As with many of the things you undertake, you'll feel better if you step back from time to time to assess how you're doing, to see what's working and what needs a little extra attention.

Try to look at your life with fresh eyes and not to judge yourself harshly. The calling to be a mom is sacred, and most moms try to be perfect.

Another Reminder: Perfection. Mom. Can't be done. Somehow it turns out right, even though many moms think they aren't doing it as well as they should.

From a mom: "I must say I often think that my children have done well despite having me for a mother." Many other moms agree. They judge themselves by a tough standard, yet beam when they talk about how incredible their children are.

When mothers speak of their lives, they know one thing. In the end, what they are proudest of, happiest about, and what they would give their lives for is their children. *Their children matter most.*

Find what works for you and how you can be the person you were called to be, to do your best and depend on God for help.

Many moms work full-time outside the home—and full-time inside the home. You are occupied with family activities and volunteer work and helping make communities better places.

Think about who you are. Are you aware of how you've changed as a mom? Are there new paths for you to venture down?

- Jot a list of words that describe you. You might even want to ask a trusted friend or family member to list words to describe you. If your children are old enough, include them in this discussion. What words would they use to describe their mom?

You can do this in a notebook or a journal or just on a scrap of paper. It doesn't have to be a big project, but it can be a huge start in knowing yourself better at this stage of your journey.

Dozens of words may pop into your mind as you think about yourself, or you may have a tough time coming up with a list. Do any of these describe you?

Thankful	Kind
Optimistic	Helpful
Angry	Useful
Tired	Purposeful
Anxious	Fun
Fearful	Friendly
Fretful	Prayerful
Happy	Playful

Make your list to see what best describes you. Try to learn more about your talents and your gifts through the way you describe yourself, or the way others who know and love you describe you.

Consider what this list says about you.

What do you like?

What do you want to change?

Remember:

You can't do everything.

Quit trying to be perfect.

Ask God for help each day.

Learn to listen for God's response.

As you think of a map for your life, start with this: Where are you going? How are you going to get there? These two questions can help you in so many ways. You can even use them each morning when you wake up, considering what is most important for the day ahead.

Clarify what you want to do. Put up a stop sign for negative thoughts that say you can't do these things.

Consider this prayer: "God, what would you have me do? How would you have me do it? What needs to change? What stays the same? What's next? I surrender my life and my family to you, and I need your help."

Life may be calm and joyful right now. Or challenges and problems may be hitting you head-on. Wherever you are, whatever your situation, start a thrilling trip.

Identify what gives you energy—and what drains your energy. Write these down without spending too much time overthinking the list. See what bubbles to the top. These will be landmarks to put on your Mom Map, things you want to see more of and things you want to avoid.

Use your famous problem-solving skills—which every mom has—to add more of the things that give you energy each day and fewer of the things that drain your energy.

Don't try to do an extreme makeover of your life all at once. Merely consider the best next step you can take—and the next and the next. Be specific as you think about the kind of mom you want to be, the kind of woman you want to be, the person God calls you to be.

Take steps toward a more meaningful life. Read a verse of scripture. Say a prayer. Develop your own Quiet Corner, a place where you can have a moment to reflect and renew. The examples at the end of each chapter can help you get started.

"It's the little things that you can change about yourself that make it easier to deal with others and life," a mother *says.*

Start here: "the little things that you can change about yourself." Set aside time each day, if possible, even if you can find only five or ten minutes. Or if you can't do it daily, do it when you can. Open up quiet in your world. Offer thanks for your blessings, and ask for help with your needs. This journey may be the most important one you ever take.

13

Mom's Quiet Corner

Busy mom's tip

"You have to learn to say no—something I am still working on. The thing that helps keep me most organized is a to-do list. I use one every day. It keeps me on track."

A mom's special scripture

"Commit to the LORD whatever you do, / and your plans will succeed" (Proverbs 16:3).

Mom to mom

"Give yourself the privilege of making a few mistakes. Set goals—they're important—but allow for the unforeseen. Give yourself the same mercy and grace that you'd give your best friend."

Prayer for the journey

Dear God, thank you for trusting me to be a mom. Help me make great decisions and be aware of your will and your guidance. Give me strength and courage, and watch over my family. In the name of Christ. Amen.

CHAPTER TWO

More Joy, Less Juggling

Know When to Say No

Encouraging Word: *You can learn to say no to too many activities.*

Everyday Step: *Trim one event from your calendar.*

*Slow down, slow down, slow down. Simplify your life
as much as possible. Learn to say no to things you
don't want to do. Learn to have fun again with simple things.
God wants us to live a joyful life, not be beaten down by it.*
—A Mom's Thoughts

Most moms know the distressing noise a washing machine makes when they put too many clothes in. That wobbling sound is downright menacing.

Most moms also know what to do when this happens: adjust the load or take something out.

So it is in life.

Moms are given clues when they overload. At times the signals are extreme. At times they are subtle. One major clue is when you find yourself living without joy too much of the time.

That's when you yield to big worry over minor things. You fret. You are grouchy. You don't have much fun with the kids. You may even get physically ill—a cold or an upset stomach, for example.

Guard your mom time.

That means taking on fewer items to juggle. This can be extremely difficult in today's hectic world, but you can learn to do so. As you figure out how to have fewer balls in the air, you find yourself with more room for joy. This opens up all sorts of new ways to be the mom—and person—you want to be.

Joy! What a remarkable word and goal for your life. Think of how you affect your family and others around you when you live with joy. Imagine the energy and enthusiasm and encouragement you bring into your home.

To find joy, you have to learn to say no. This is tough, particularly for moms.

Everywhere I turn, people need help saying no. Because they agree to do too much, they overload and wind up doing things that wear them out and take them away from priorities. They even shortchange their families when they say yes to the wrong things.

Start simply.

Try guidelines such as those you use with your children to help yourself begin—encouraging, loving, assembling what you need to move forward. Don't fret about what other people do or think. Be true to yourself and your family and the life God calls you to live. Trade guilt for prayer.

As you begin, you may feel as though you are looking in one of those magnifying mirrors that shows all your flaws. That's an overblown image that puts too much attention on the problems and not enough on what's right. You have a blemish or two, a wrinkle here and there. But you also have innumerable blessings and the beauty of creating a family.

Try this: Life as a mom is full of *shoulds*, all those things you think you should be doing on any given day. Begin to replace those with *coulds*, the many things you could do to live more meaningfully. "Shoulda. Coulda. Woulda. I don't want to hear it," says one working mom of three children ranging from a toddler to a preteen.

Need to "No"

Remember: When you say no to one thing, you say yes to something else. By saying no to an extra committee or one too many lunch dates or an extra errand or a shopping trip, you say yes to dinner with your family or time to read a book. By saying no to chitchat at the office, you might say yes to finish a project more quickly so you can get home sooner.

You can also do things on a "need to no" basis. Say no because you need to—because you are tired or have too much coming up in one season or your children seem to need extra care.

Keep an Eye on Your Calendar

If only moms could learn to guard their calendars the way they guard their children. Just think about how that could change

KEEPING CONTROL OF YOUR CALENDAR REQUIRES CONSTANT VIGILANCE. YOU MAY BE SHOCKED AT HOW QUICKLY YOUR CALENDAR FILLS UP IF YOU ARE NOT PAYING ATTENTION.

your life. You've probably used "the grip" in a crowded place where you want your child right by your side. Or you've been to a playground or other public place where your eyes never stray from your child. Your schedule needs that watchful eye.

Keeping control of your calendar requires constant vigilance. You may be shocked at how quickly your calendar fills up if you are not paying attention. Activities and appointments and all manner of things sneak up on you. Your schedule gets too crowded, and you become increasingly tired, worried, and annoyed with those around you. In addition to managing homes and activities, moms juggle many relationships, all of which take time and energy.

How to Guard Your Mom Time

- Pray about your commitments.
- Set a goal for time you will spend with your children.
- Focus on your family as a priority on your calendar.

- Avoid time-wasting distractions. Ask yourself: *Is this the highest and best use of my time?*

- Consider the season of time you are in, the ages of your children and how much attention they need from you.

- Take on fewer activities, especially ongoing standing meetings and obligations that will take you away from home when you need to be with your children.

- Be disciplined about adding activities to your calendar.

- Be careful to avoid doing things because you feel that you're letting someone else down, you're not doing your share, or you're the only one who can do that particular assignment the right way.

- Be consistent. Figure out what you want and need to spend your time on, and let your calendar reflect that.

- Factor in fun time with your family and for yourself. The former will build stronger relationships; the latter will give you more energy.

- Look for ways to use your time to bring joy to others, in your family, at church, at work, in your neighborhood, and in each of your daily encounters. A smile makes a difference in most situations. "A cheerful look brings joy to the heart," says Proverbs 15:30. And another reminder from Scriptures: "Let the light of your face shine upon us, O LORD. / You have filled my heart with greater joy / than when their grain and new wine abound. / I will lie down and sleep in peace, / for you alone, O LORD, / make me dwell in safety" (Psalm 4:6-8).

Moms like to get everything in order. They want the dishes washed, the kitchen mopped. Before a trip, they're making lists and packing and repacking. But the joy of daily life can come in going with the flow, open to the opportunity that presents itself, whether to get down on the floor and play with their child or to go out as a family for pizza. They have to say no to one planned thing to say yes to spontaneity.

Don't Miss a Precious Mom Moment

Mom moments appear regularly—and they can easily be missed in a hectic day. These small, subtle moments enrich a mom's soul, maybe even bring a tear of joy to her eye.

As an amateur birdwatcher, I compare these moments to the male cardinal and the female cardinal. The male is bright red and stands out against the bare branches of winter, almost startling in his beauty. The female is much duller at first glance, until you notice her beautiful beak, a shade that reminds me of the red-orange crayon I enjoyed as a child. It would be so easy to overlook the beauty of the female cardinal, just as it so easy to overlook small, tender moments of being a mom, those minutes or even seconds that make your heart want to pop with joy.

Becoming observant helps you notice more. This skill builds on itself. That means being in the moment, not letting your mind race to the thousands of things you need to be doing or replaying something that happened earlier in the day. You might see your preschool daughter sitting by the window because her doll "wants to watch the snow." Or your kindergartener explaining to a younger brother why big heels are important on cowboy boots. Or your middle schooler helping a young cousin choose a book to read. Savor the sentimentality of being a parent to bring a different kind of joy, one that shores up your spirit for the rough days and gives you hope as you go about your life.

"I do not want to miss one of my daughter's breathless runs around our yard or my son's silly, toothless 'kisses' that he is just learning to give," says a working mom who juggles joyfully and tries to follow her priorities each day.

Mom moments can be pure and simple, such as an observation about a precious baby boy in my family. As he was getting close to walking, his young parents proudly announced, "They say he's the fastest crawler in the entire church nursery." The smallest joys, the biggest smiles!

Subtleties can also help you be aware when your child needs you in a special way and cut down on your fear of missing those needs.

From a mom: "You have to take this parenting thing one day at a time, and *always* trust your gut instincts. I call it 'Mommy radar.' Mommies just know when something isn't right with their children." Don't say yes to so many things that your "radar" malfunctions.

To Pay Attention, to Ignore

A regular aggravation for many mothers is dealing with car problems and deciding how serious they are. These problems provide an illustration for decisions you make each day. In the midst of writing this book, the "check engine" light lit up on my car. While I thought it was probably only a maintenance reminder, I couldn't help thinking about a young friend who had ignored such a light a few weeks earlier—and burned up the motor in her mom's car.

Your quest as a mom may be similar to this. Every now and then the "check engine" light will come on in your life. When you are restless or unsettled, you will need to decide whether it is major (engine about to blow) or something that you can take care of easily (tighten that gas cap, ma'am).

Consider your daily life, what you need to pay attention to and what you need to ignore.

Moms share the feeling that their busyness is just too much to handle and that they are shortchanging themselves and their children. This layer of worry shows up in different ways and makes life tougher. You can figure out what works best for you.

Remember, you can't do everything.

As you seek, you will begin to find what is most important to you. Then you must decide what you can ignore, what you want to toss out, and what you want to hold close.

Your challenge will be to discern what you need to trim from your schedule and what you need to add, to begin to know when things sort of aren't right or *really* aren't right, when they may need a little tweaking or when a major overhaul is called for. Take it a day at a time, a decision at a time.

Ask for help from others, especially your spouse or someone you can depend on.

"I have to give a lot of credit to my husband," says the mom of two college students. "In many households, it's the mom who does all of the juggling. It is so helpful when it's not just one spouse making all of the sacrifices. My husband was always available to talk with them and help them with homework and projects late in the night when I faded out."

Maybe you roll your eyes here because your spouse does not help in ways you feel you need. Talk with him about it. If necessary, see a professional counselor or speak with your pastor together to build a stronger relationship that works in your active lives.

If you are a single or widowed parent, look for other moms you can share duties with. Help each other with chores and errands and child care to make the juggling easier. Call on your family members. Develop a network of support.

While subtracting certain activities, consider what might need adding to give you more energy or patience. For certain moms this is exercise. For others it is serving others. There are many possibilities.

This seems to go against learning to say no, but living fully means taking care of yourself and others. Each person is called on to love and to help. Perhaps you don't have time to volunteer frequently or can't do as much as you would like during a particular season of time. However, you will get energy and inspire your children as you open up your calendar for kindness and service.

From a mom: "I feel called to serve the community. . . . I feel I must contribute in some way to bring the gospel to life. It is not enough for me to just take care of my family's needs. Yes, my family is my God-given priority, but I feel compelled to reach beyond myself and help in whatever way I can. Granted, this often feels like a teeny tiny drop in the bucket, and I am often tempted to despair that it is ineffective wasted time that I cannot afford. But this is exactly the kindness that is needed by those who live in darkness. I can only plant the seeds, and God will help them grow. I pray God will bless my efforts, and I know I may never see the fruits of my labor. I pray that my example will teach my children to care for others."

What's right for you at this point in life?

Many mothers struggle with the need for more time with their children, and moms disagree on the right amount of time. This is a good place to recall that every family is different and that you'll need to find what works best for you. Maybe you work full-time outside the home and plan and focus to have great times with your children, but spend fewer hours with them. Or perhaps you set aside evenings and weekends for them. You might be a mom who stays at home and tries to be available most of the time. This varies. Do what works for you.

Take a clear look at these questions:

How much time do you spend with your children?

Does that time fill you up and help you meet your children's needs?

Are there changes you need to make? Activities you might give up to have more time?

Is it possible you are focusing *too* much on your children and not taking care of yourself?

Moms try so hard to get it all right that they rarely relax, and they find joy to be elusive. Are you pushing too hard? Do you expect too much of yourself and others?

Yes, you want to be and do your best. And you want your children to be and do their best. But there is a fine line here that can head toward perfectionism. As the mother of two young sons says, "Don't expect too much from your kids. They aren't little adults. They're kids, and kids by their very nature do stupid stuff. It's how they learn. Try to keep a reasonable perspective."

Calling All Night Owls

As your children get older, you will have different expectations of them. Allow time to listen to them, even when they let you down or fall short of what you wanted for them. This often means shaving something off your schedule, but it can offer joy from knowing you did your best.

A mom in a large family, with children from preschool to college, says that with her teens, she must take extra time to know what is going on with them and to determine what is behind their behavior. That often includes late-night talks or conversations in the car. "If you can make yourself be a night owl," she says, "you can get a lot of good conversation."

Technology can be a terrible distraction in this effort. "I think cell phones are completely disruptive for relationships with children," says a mom. It is tough to keep the phone from interfering with joyful moments, with children or when you are alone. Maybe this is one area where you need to say no more frequently in your own life.

"I feel like quality and quantity time with children are equally important," says a stay-at-home mom. "We all need a break sometime, but I often find this mentality of getting away from the kids as a cop-out to the responsibility of raising a little person. . . . I also think it is important to be mentally present to our children when they need us, not just physically present. This is another daunting challenge." "The bottom line is keep life simple," says a mom who works part-time and has three children, including a toddler.

Another reminder from the Bible: "This day is sacred to our Lord. Do not grieve, for the joy of the LORD is your strength" (Nehemiah 8:10).

"Whatever you are dealing with at the moment will soon be a memory," says a mom. "Yes, the children may drive you crazy. Yes, it may seem that all you do is dishes and laundry, but if you can laugh and have fun and tease and joke about things while you are solving a problem, it makes things a lot easier. Surrounding yourself with joyful people is huge."

The amount of activity that is right for you and your family will depend on you and your family. But most moms overload. Overdo. Overschedule. And then they freak out. They wobble like the washing machine.

You can find joy in so many places, in so many ways. But you will have to say no along the way and give the boot to guilt.

May you be able to say, as this verse does: "My joy knows no bounds" (2 Corinthians 7:4).

What brings you joy today as a mom? What do you need to say no to?

Mom's Quiet Corner

Busy mom's tip

"Children have such happy hearts, and they love it when their mom is playing anything with them."

A mom's special scripture

"Train a child in the way he should go, / and when he is old he will not turn from it" (Proverbs 22:6).

Mom to mom

"Living life to the fullest means enjoying life. Enjoy your family, enjoy your job, and enjoy your friends. God has blessed us with so many things that we take for granted. We should enjoy life while we are in it."

Prayer for the journey

Dear God, thank you for the gift of my family. Help me see joy in each day. Help me spread joy to my children and others around me. In your holy name. Amen.

CHAPTER THREE

The Promise of Peace

Awareness of the Goodness of Life

Encouraging Word: *Peace of mind is possible for you.*

Everyday Step: *Choose one way to turn
down the noise in your daily life.*

*The most peace I feel is when I remember
that God is in control, not me.*
—A Mom's Thoughts

On certain days, life can seem like being in the midst of a
drive-through car wash. When the day ends, you breathe a
sigh of relief. As with all that soap and water and noise and
automation, everything turned out okay.

This is the way peace sometimes feels. You wait to pass through
the commotion to the end and hope you aren't swallowed up by
all the activity around you.

Gather a group of women and ask them what they want in life. *Peace* will often be near the top of the list. Moms long for peace. In their daily lives, this means a calmer spirit. It means a more patient attitude. It means not being frenzied. It means a moment of quiet in a noisy day, a calm certainty that they are making the right decisions and issues will work out well.

Living peacefully may seem elusive. But it is possible if you make daily decisions that support your peaceful priority.

Pursuing peace in your daily life brings a bonus. It helps you be more joyful. When you are more joyful, you will be more peaceful. It's a tremendous payoff that builds on itself.

Peaceful moms are often joyful moms. They are comfortable in their own skins and find happiness in little ways. They give thanks each and every day for their families and for their blessings, large and small.

They aren't angels or superheroes. They get frustrated like everyone else. But they are learning to relax and trust God when the road is rocky. They try not to think one thing and do another, but let their actions line up with their priorities.

Consider these words from Isaiah 55:12: "You will go out in joy / and be led forth in peace." Joy and peace. Together. In your life.

Logistics of Life, Peaceful Resolutions

Living with a peaceful spirit is not easy with heavy schedules, the logistics of everyday life, and unexpected troubles that pop up from day to day.

Many moms rely on God's help as the foundation for their peace and for how they get through their days, knowing that life can spin them around and shake them up.

From a mom: "When you put God first in your life, the rest just falls into place." How do you do that? This favorite Scripture passage, mentioned by many happy moms, serves as a guide:

> Be glad in the Lord always! Again I say, be glad! Let your gentleness show in your treatment of all people. The Lord is near. Don't be anxious about anything; rather bring up all your requests to God in your prayers and petitions, along with giving thanks. Then the peace of God that exceeds all understanding will keep your hearts and minds safe in Christ Jesus. (Philippians 4:4-7 CEB)

This passage outlines basic steps that have wondrous results in the peace department and in living an overall less hurried and less worried life:

Be glad.

Be gentle.

Know that God is with you.

Don't worry.

Pray, asking God for what you need.

Offer thanks for your blessings. Your many blessings. The very good things that happen in your life, with your family, for big things and little things and all those in between.

For peace to find its way into your daily life, turn down the volume on your noisy world. This means saying no to noise and yes to more time sitting quietly. Say no to watching TV, no to talking on the telephone, no to tapping on the computer. Consider ways in your life to be still and hear the guidance of God.

One Technique: Set aside a few minutes for a "quiet break."

From a mom: "I occasionally sit and 'breathe' a few minutes, just to regroup. It might be immediately after the children leave for school, after the hectic rush of the morning. Or it could be just before they return home, before the storm of homework and dinner preparation begins. Taking a small break will often provide just the spark needed to get through the next phase of the day."

Find moments here or there. While it would be nice to have a spa vacation or a silent retreat, you probably aren't going to work those in on a regular basis. Perhaps you've told your family, "I need a little peace and quiet." Consider how those two words work together. When you are constantly surrounded by noise and activity, peace may seem out of reach. When I sit quietly at home, I am struck by just how hurried and noisy my life becomes bit by bit. I need to slow it down more. And more. And quiet it again.

Reminder: You need quiet at times to develop peace. The word *calm* goes along with this. That doesn't mean your life is dull or your household boring. It means that the atmosphere around you is not always frantic, that you don't overschedule or fret all the time that things aren't just so.

Daily Choices for Peace

Among the many choices you make each day will be the times when you can choose drama and anger or peace. Don't let yourself be drawn into battles that have no reason to involve you.

Making your way through each day, let some things slide. Remember the instructions from Philippians 4: "Let your gentleness show in your treatment of all people."

Maybe you are thinking that this whole peace business comes from a deep spiritual core that you don't have. Not true!

You can embrace it with very ordinary, maybe even unexpected, steps:

- **Quit speeding. Sounds easy enough, right?** All that rushing doesn't help you get where you're going much more quickly, and it destroys your calm. Besides, it's against the law and dangerous.

- **Don't get mad at other drivers, even if you think they are going too slow or should have gone through that yellow light.**

- **Tune out excessive news coverage of contentious topics.** Who can be peaceful if they listen to people quarrel all day and night on cable television or talk radio?

- **Don't be drawn into arguments with a colleague at work.** These are not unlike squabbles between children over who gets to ride in the front seat or whose turn it is to clean off the table. Be bigger than that. This doesn't mean you are a doormat or a blah person. Instead, look at things with a more positive, gentle approach. Be the cheerful person with the smile instead of the grouch for whom life is one hassle after another. The latter is not fertile soil for peacefulness.

- **Depend on your children to help cut down on worries.** From a mom: "Teach your kids about home safety, public safety, and stranger danger. Kids who know exactly what to do, and then do it, spare you a lot of stress."

- **Toss out self-pity.** Avoid the grumpy-victim mentality— the idea that you are put upon and taken for granted, that nothing gets done if you don't do it. Or it gets done but it doesn't get done right or that you have no control over your schedule and never get to do what you want to do. Certainly most people have days when they feel sorry for themselves. Maybe it's a flat tire or a bounced check, a misunderstanding with a child or a spat with a spouse. But beware letting that take over your attitude and then your behavior. Pray about it. Talk issues over with your spouse or child or a trusted friend. Listen to their feedback. Take a hard look at how you react to ordinary situations, and see if you need to make adjustments.

- **Think of the privilege of parenthood and the many good things that come your way.** Maybe you need to not let little things bug you or perhaps ask your family to help out more. Neglect a chore for playtime with a child, knowing that a little extra dust may bother you but won't be the end of the world. Extra fun with your family can put a song in your heart and help you go to sleep that night with a feeling of contentment.

Maybe you find it tough to find peace because of regrets from the past. The "if onlys" of our lives can make us unsettled and uncertain. Pray for God's help, forgive yourself, and allow God to forgive you.

At times, however, you can't shake anxiety or nervousness. If you are depressed or overly anxious, do not hesitate to get professional help. Maybe you hold yourself up against the standards of others and feel ashamed or unworthy or that you should be able to find the peace that eludes you. Turn to a trained counselor or pastor. Such resources can be blessings that help put you on the path where you want to be.

- **Read the Bible more regularly to find increased peace.** God will speak to you in unexpected ways, through ancient words with modern truths. You will become familiar with verses that pop into your mind during tumultuous times, scriptures that steady you when you are blown about.

Psalm 25 brings comfort and peace to many. "To you, O LORD, I lift up my soul. / O my God, in you I trust; do not let me be put to shame; / do not let my enemies exult over me," say verses 1-2 (NRSV). As one mother and grandmother says, "This is a choral anthem that my son learned in high school. When I read the passage, I can hear the chorus singing. Other verses in the same psalm are very comforting. Many of them are highlighted in bright pink in my Bible. Among those: 'Relieve the troubles of my heart, / and bring me out of my distress. / Consider my affliction and my trouble, / and forgive all my sins. . . . / O guard my life, and deliver me; / do not let me be put to shame, for I take refuge in you'" (Psalm 25:17-18, 20 NRSV).

Finding time to read the Bible can be hard, but it pays off. "Bible reading can be the easiest thing to put aside when you're busy, but the results of reading are huge," says a mom. Reading and studying God's word offer her strength and peace and help her refocus. One way she grows is by listening to online sermons.

Rejoice!

From the words of Philippians above, one aspect of finding peace is learning to rejoice in all that God gives you. Take inventory to see if you're grateful for the good in each day.

As a mom, you've probably had one of those "say thank you" moments. Your child gets a gift or receives a compliment and stands there without saying a word. "Tell her thank you," you urge. "Say thank you." You feel embarrassed and look sheepish and wish an enthusiastic expression of gratitude would pour out of your child's mouth. As your children get older, even as adults, you may nag them to write thank-you notes and are thrilled when they jot a note for a gift.

Unfortunately, often moms get so rushed that they overlook things they should be saying thanks for. They are like their children when they happily accept a gift or a compliment but forget to say thanks. The more they hurry, the more likely they are to let blessings slip by unnoticed or underappreciated. It's shockingly easy to live that way—forgetting to say thank you to God, for all the blessings that are showered upon you, and to the people around you for all they do for you.

This gratitude opens the door to finding peace on even the craziest days. Take today, for example. What happened that was good? Even if it didn't rank up there in the all-star days, surely something good still happened. "Let the peace of Christ rule in your hearts. . . . And be thankful" (Colossians 3:15).

I am blessed by a group of women known as the "Barret Girls," friends since Barret Elementary School days, now nearly five decades. Our bond is enhanced by our love and memories of one another's mothers. A warm feeling runs through us as we recall the friendships our mothers shared and how those women treated each of us. What shone in those moms when I was a child now glows in their daughters as they love their children.

Mothers pass on wonderful attributes to their children. You are doing that. Never forget it.

One of these longtime friends has a teenage son, a child born when she was thirty-four, and she shares how she learned to be thankful and focus on what mattered: "As with all moms, you make countless decisions every day. What guided me the most was relying on the love and support of family and close friends. I was trying so hard to make everything perfect for my new baby that I lost sight of what was important. The best advice I got was from a very close friend. She said, 'You know your baby doesn't care what he's wearing; he doesn't care what day care he goes to; he doesn't care if he has the most fashionable baby furniture. Your baby boy doesn't care if his pediatrician is the "it" doctor in town. Your son just wants to be loved and cared for by you and his father, and the rest will take care of itself.' This advice gave me pause, and I began to focus on what was important and enjoy the wonderful blessing I had been given."

The Power of a Thankful Heart

To find peace in motherhood, a thankful heart is vital. It will help you get through the toughest days. You will see your children with new eyes, appreciating what they offer in your life each day. This attitude of praise will be passed along to your children, a positive way to look at the world and to appreciate what they have.

The astonishing thing about a thankful heart is that it crowds out worry. There's just not room for both. So if you want to worry less, say thank you more. To top it off, while peace goes hand in hand with joy, it also goes hand in hand with thankfulness.

Christ watches over your life and the lives of your family members, a deep well from which to draw thanksgiving. "For he will command his angels concerning you / to guard you in all your ways" (Psalm 91:11 NRSV). Consider what that means in your daily life. God will help you through dark places. He will give you wisdom. He will answer your prayers. He will provide peace.

As a guide for daily focus, take a look at this apt verse from 2 Timothy 1: "I know the one in whom I've placed my trust. I'm convinced that God is powerful enough to protect what he has placed in my trust until that day. . . . Protect this good thing that has been placed in your trust through the Holy Spirit who lives in us" (v. 12, 14 CEB).

Those few words offer a way to build upon the blessings of each day:

- *Believe.* **That beautifully simple word can change your perspective each day.**

- **Make a list of what you will entrust to the Lord for the day.** Identify your priorities each morning. What do you want to spend your time and energy on? What does God have for you to do? In what ways does your family most need you on this particular day?
- **Hand those topics to God.** Imagine a loving God guarding those things. When you begin to rush or fret, remember your priorities. Decide what needs to be trimmed and how to handle the situation.
- **Regain energy by remembering that you have a divine guard to help you through the day, your own holy assistant to walk with you.** This approach lessens worry immensely.

One of the lakes in North Louisiana, near where we live, is clogged with an invasive plant, choking out other life in the lake. One peaceful Saturday morning I watched as an injured goose tried to make its way across the shallow lake, tangled in the weeds. He persevered even when I was certain he was so tired he could never make it. It wasn't pretty, but he reached the peninsula he was aiming for and seemed to relax immediately.

Sometimes you get to peace the hard way. You struggle. You cry while you pray for peace that passes understanding. You argue with God—and others. It's like tossing and turning in bed at night, unable to get comfortable. But take a deep breath and pray for peace. Pray every day for peace. Many times a day if needed.

Take this day as a gift. Begin to relax.

- **Be anxious for nothing, the Bible says.**
  Be anxious for nothing.
  Be *anxious* for nothing.
  Be anxious for *nothing.*

Surrender your anxiety to God. Know that God's arms are wrapped around you in the same way that you comfort your own child.

"May you have more and more grace and peace through the knowledge of God and Jesus our Lord" (2 Peter 1:2 CEB).

Mom's Quiet Corner

Busy mom's tip

"Little things like making cookies or playing a board game go a long way with my daughter. It doesn't take long, but we laugh out loud and then she tells people about it for a few days afterward. We both look forward to those times."

> SURRENDER YOUR ANXIETY TO GOD. KNOW THAT GOD'S ARMS ARE WRAPPED AROUND YOU IN THE SAME WAY THAT YOU COMFORT YOUR OWN CHILD.

A mom's special scripture

"Therefore, humble yourselves under God's power so that

he may raise you up in the last day. Throw all your anxiety onto him, because he cares about you" (1 Peter 5:6-7 CEB).

Mom to mom

"Worry does not add to my life, so I don't indulge in it. I am not in control; God is, and I can trust him. Scriptures back that up, and I repeat those to myself when I start to worry."

Prayer for the journey

Dear God, who watches over me and my family, I ask that you help calm my heart and soothe my concerns, that you help me learn not to worry but to trust you. Lord, I thank you for hearing this prayer. In your name. Amen.

CHAPTER FOUR

Parenting Priorities

Blueprint for Meaningful Mom Moments

Encouraging Word: *You know what is most important in your life.*

Everyday Step: *Offer a kindness here and there.*

> *One of the simplest, yet most rewarding, ways to live*
> *life to the full is to concentrate on the needs of others.*
> *Focusing on helping others takes your mind off*
> *your own problems and keeps things in perspective.*
> —A Mom's Thoughts

B etty Pace was born in 1924, way out in the country in North Louisiana. She died unexpectedly in 1977 but left her mark on the world because she lived by her priorities— faith, the way she treated others, and the way she loved and taught her children.

She was my wonderful mother. She did not go to college, and I suspect she never made a list of priorities. But you always knew what was important to her.

That, in a nutshell, is the way parenting priorities work. You figure out what is most important to you, and you make daily decisions that support those priorities. You make many choices. If things don't go as hoped, you keep living by what matters most.

If you examine your mother's or grandmother's life or that of another mom who is special to you, you can find lessons you want to live by and see what works and what doesn't. For my mother, these were clear: Love. Pray. Trust. Laugh. Be kind to others.

What's Most Important

Priorities often become vague and merge into one overpowering to-do list. Instead, consider reminding yourself of What's Most Important. You know what matters to you, even if you let it slip occasionally or have forsaken it altogether. Take time to revisit what matters most to you and what you need to do to live accordingly.

"I know that mothers today live a hectic lifestyle," says a friend of many years. "However, my mother was a single parent raising five children, working two jobs at times, but she managed to live faithfully and enjoy her life. It wasn't easy, but I think discipline was the mainstay of her life. She never lost sight of what was important to her."

One of those priorities: "My mom was a devout Christian. Every Sunday she would get us all up; we would dress up and walk to Sunday school and church. When we were very young children, if we couldn't attend church, she would provide it at home. We sang hymns and she would teach us a Sunday school lesson. She loved God and never failed to thank him for everything she had. Her faith truly did sustain her throughout her life."

Your core beliefs can shape your daily decisions and help you be the mom you want to be. A former coworker and her husband rely on a favorite scripture that helps define their priorities as a family: "But as for me and my household, we will serve the LORD" (Joshua 24:15). "Friends gave it to us in a framed presentation when we got married," she says. Later, many states away, they bought a home that had the scripture engraved on a small plaque by the door. "While there are endless lyrical and inspirational quotes in the Bible that can evoke the whole spectrum of emotions, this—to us—brings it down to its simplest form."

What brings your beliefs as a mom to their simplest form?

What words might you list as reminders of your priorities?

Stay Focused

So often in a mom's life, it is difficult to stay focused on What's Most Important because you are drawn off course by an errand, a household crisis, an unexpected work assignment, a child's misbehavior in public, or any one of a thousand distractions.

Being faithful as a mom—living meaningfully—takes many forms, and one of these is not to be rushed and harried too much of the time. You may lose your focus and rush from time to time. But make decisions to slow it down when that becomes a pattern.

Suggestions:

- **Don't be afraid to shift your daily priorities as needed.** "If you feel like kicking back to enjoy your child and family, even though work calls," says a mom, "take the time to enjoy the family. Then get back to work, knowing you may have to put off a household task to get the job done. The point here is to make the choice to take on certain tasks, even if that means putting others on hold. And don't beat yourself up over it."
- **Know that your priorities may not be the same as everyone else's.** Find what suits your family.

"My children can testify that I didn't always keep a neat house. That was just not that important," says a mother whose daughters are in college. "I do regret we didn't have more times when our family sat down for meals at the dining table—only at holidays or when we ate out, it seems. Sometimes even church got in the way of meal times and family activities, but I accepted it without pushing it. My children always enjoyed choir and mission activities."

- **Be aware of distractions in your life, and work on efficient steps to handle them.** Some are necessary—the call from the school that your child has a fever. Others are distractions you open the door to, such as spending too much time online or being tied to your cell phone or e-mail.

- **Frequently assess priorities.** A businesswoman mentions the importance of following up on Big Picture thinking. "There are Big Picture Thinkers and Big Picture Doers," she says.

Which are you? Do you see the Big Picture for your life but can't quite work toward it? Are you a Big Picture Doer, who matches What's Most Important with everyday steps?

- **Become a Big Picture Mom.** Have hope and a vision. Many parents have vague dreams and goals for their families, but they don't take time to clarify them. Thus, they and their children drift. Pause and reflect on what you want, building hope as you go along. Reflect on the past as a guide to figure out what you want in the future.
- **Consider what you have built into your life that adds to hurry and worry.** You have the best intentions and then overload when you lose focus.

Many times through the years I have had to stop and figure out why I keep adding things—and what needs to go. I expect you will too. Make it a point to look at this intently from time to time. If you don't think you have a spare moment, do it on your lunch break or when the children are in bed. Ignore that load of laundry for one more day. Let something else go if needed. Taking time for setting priorities can make a *huge* difference in your mom days ahead.

A key step in slowing down is identifying "those other things." The things that you think you must do but really don't have to do. Or those things that aren't as important as something else. List changes that you could make to slow down, to worry less. If you'll take a few minutes and do this exercise, homing in on what matters most, you will make great strides in living as a meaningful mom.

When I was forty, I decided to run a marathon—26.2 miles, about twenty-six times farther than I could run at the time. I made up my mind, told a few folks, and set out for the weekly training runs. I am a slow runner, and most of the time the others in the training group left me behind in a matter of minutes. But it didn't matter. I found my pace, and step by step, mile by mile, I trained. I ran two marathons that year. Twenty-six miles seemed like a long way, but I took the advice of an experienced runner. I ran them one mile at a time.

Behold the mom journey. Commit to what you are *willing* to do to hurry less and to worry less. Take action. Do it bit by bit. You won't know how to do it all at once. Your strength will grow, though, through the months and years. You'll get better, and it'll sometimes seem easier and sometimes seem harder. But you'll move forward.

Not that hard a question: What do I want?

Much harder: Am I willing to do whatever it takes to accomplish it?

- **Make good communication a priority.** Consider how that looks in your daily life as a mom. An excellent, simple guide for this can be found in James 1:19: "Everyone should be quick to listen, slow to speak, and slow to grow angry" (CEB).

Be mindful of how you communicate. Do you listen?

Listening pays off in relationships with your family, with friends and other relationships, with God, and with yourself. Often moms can find answers to tough questions through listening. Those answers often bring peace.

"Part of being available is being willing to listen—without interruption or interjection of your own thoughts," says the mother of adult children and young grandchildren. However, she adds, "Be careful when offering advice to adult children! I try not to unless asked. I try to point out things my child may not have considered, to lead her thinking, rather than impose my conclusion on her. She needs to make her own decisions, but she may not have a clear idea of what her options are."

- **Spend time together as a family, assessing how much time you want and need together.** "Make the time you spend together special," says a mom, and that is true whether you all have many commitments that draw you away from home or whether you spend hours together each day.

How much time are you spending? This often depends on your family. Some people think less is better if it is quality time. Others think you need to spend more time. Decide what works for you.

- **Look for ways to have meals together.** Many moms say that having meals together makes a big difference in their family life. It comes up again and again in conversations with mothers.

"I believe that gathering together frequently as a family to share a meal is so important to family life. It never ceases to amaze me what beautiful things come forth as we stop and meet around the table to eat," says a young mom. "But meal planning and prep do not come naturally or easily for me. Therefore, I have to work very hard at it. I often say to myself, 'I may not love to cook, but I dearly love the people who eat at my table.' I am so jealous of those who can cook with grace and ease or find it 'therapeutic,' but I know the dividends will be more than worth it in the end. Mealtime is important not only to families but also communities. After all, what did Christ himself give us and leave for us to remember him and to bring us together as a family—a supper!"

- **Show mercy to those you encounter—your children and grandchildren, your coworkers and other moms around you, aware of those who hurt.** A grandmother offers these words for moms to consider when children are going through difficult situations: "You offer unconditional love, that all-important listening ear, time spent doing things together, encouragement and, yes, discipline, because when their worlds are turned upside down stability is most needed. Children are adaptable and resilient, but not without proper attention and care. You just can't let them fumble around, trying to find their own solutions."

- **Take time for individuals—a child, your spouse or partner, your own mom, or a close friend.** When you are overloaded, it is much harder to do this. You lean toward group activities and the crowd. This becomes a form of multitasking, meeting the needs of several people at once. This clearly shifts through the years. When your children are younger, you may find less time for visits with friends, for example. If you're a single mom, you may want to pray about your adult relationships, where you spend your time, and how to balance the needs of your children against your own needs.

From a mom: "I think relationships are important, not only with your mate and God, but also with other women. Nurture those relationships, and they will nurture you."

"Making it a top priority to set aside time and energy to be directed to my husband is so important," says another mother. "This is hard to do when you have four children but not impossible. Real love is not a feeling but a decision. I can see how easily and often this priority can slip behind the job of raising children. But as moms, we can give no greater gift to our children than to become a conscious channel of grace for our husbands by actively deciding to love, help, support, and attend to them."

"I have friends who I have watched simply grow apart from their spouses. They got to a place in their lives where they have grown apart because they didn't keep doing things together and

> DON'T GO TO
> CHURCH BECAUSE YOU
> FEEL THAT YOU HAVE
> TO. GO TO FILL UP
> YOUR SPIRIT AND TO
> ADD TO YOUR ENERGY
> AND WISDOM AS A
> MOM.

didn't develop common interests," says the mother of three. "Obviously they started out with things in common, but because they didn't keep working at it, they grew apart. I feel like the same thing can happen with your children. As our children get older, if we don't continue to do things that interest and involve them, then they will not want to spend time with us, and it will be that much harder to develop those relationships later."

- **Become part of a community of faith.** Attend church. Go to worship, and choose small groups that help you grow and also allow you a place to express your needs and challenges.

"Sunday church fuels my spirit," says one mom. "It is not an obligation for me; it is a privilege. It is one place where I know I am *exactly* where I am supposed to be. Very often my heart soars in the knowledge of this freedom. It is a joy to worship."

By the weekend, moms may feel too tired to go to church or need to take care of chores or errands, and finding a way to attend church can take a course correction. Don't go to church because you feel that you have to. Go to fill up your spirit and to add to your energy and wisdom as a mom. If worship feels like another thing on your to-do list, change your viewpoint. You will be renewed; you will see people who care about you and your family, and those who need your touch. Look forward to time to catch your breath and refresh your thoughts.

"We talk a lot about parenting in our Sunday school class," says a mother of four. Such a class allows you to hear the opinions of others and share your thoughts.

"Guard your steps when you go to the house of God. . . . Do not be quick with your mouth, / do not be hasty in your heart / to utter anything before God. / God is in heaven / and you are on earth, / so let your words be few. . . . Stand in awe of God" (Ecclesiastes 5:1-2, 7).

- **Reflect on Jesus and his call to the disciples as you consider your priorities.** "As Jesus passed alongside the Sea of Galilee, he saw two brothers, Simon and Andrew, throwing fishing nets into the sea, for they were fishermen. 'Come, follow me,' he said, 'and I'll show you how to fish for people.' Right away, they left their nets and followed him" (Mark 1:16-18 CEB).

Jesus said, "Follow me," and they did. They didn't make lists and do all sorts of planning. They just followed. The outcome would be the greatest adventure of their lives, full of miracles. They would be changed, and they would help change the world forever.

As moms try to live by what is most important, the answer starts here. Follow Christ. The model he outlines in the Bible answers so many parenting priorities—loving others, treating people the way you want to be treated, serving, bearing fruit that lasts.

Relax and savor your precious children.

"I have to get a grip on my schedule," says a working mother. "You can beat yourself up too much. If we would do what the Bible tells us for our lives, we'd be better mothers."

Think about these words:

> The LORD is my rock, my fortress, and my deliverer,
>   my God, my rock, in whom I take refuge,
> my shield and the horn of my salvation,
>   my stronghold and my refuge,
>   my savior; you save me from violence.
> I call upon the LORD, who is worthy to be praised.
> (2 Samuel 22:2-4 NRSV)

Mom's Quiet Corner

Busy mom's tip

"The number one lesson I learned was from a teacher friend. We were having lunch with her two-year-old daughter when the daughter started misbehaving. My friend whispered something in her ear, and the little girl started behaving. I asked, 'What did you say to her?' My friend gave her daughter two choices. The girl chose to sit down rather than have to leave. Simple as that!"

A mom's special scripture

Do not fear, for I have redeemed you;

I have called you by name, you are mine.

When you pass through the waters, I will be with you;

and through the rivers, they shall not overwhelm you;

when you walk through fire you shall not be burned,

and the flame shall not consume you.

For I am the LORD your God. (Isaiah 43:1-3 NRSV)

Mom to mom

"One of my goals this year is to volunteer more. I find it makes me feel good inside to give back. I know God wants us to be mindful of others less fortunate than ourselves. I've discovered when we focus on others instead of ourselves so much, we hurry less and worry less."

Prayer for the journey

Dear loving God, please place people on my path and help me see their needs. Give me energy and kindness to help them. Let me always show my children the importance of mercy and kindness toward others. I pray in the name of Christ. Amen.

CHAPTER FIVE

Building a Hopeful Heart

Expect Great Things to Unfold

Encouraging Word: *Wonderful things will occur in life.*

Everyday Step: *Set a small positive goal for your week.*

Most of us get so caught up in one way or another about the appearance of having it all that we forget to thank God and be grateful for all the ways we are blessed every day.
—A Mom's Thoughts

Moms are by nature hopeful creatures. They hope for good grades, wise decisions, and even excellent careers for their children. They hope their kids will behave in church. They hope their children won't hang out with the wrong crowd. Or come home with green hair. Most of this boils down to one thing: moms hope for the best for their children.

As with many parts of motherhood, hope ebbs and flows. One day you are buoyed by optimism and courage. The next day you feel weak, your hope swamped by fear. As you contemplate living fully as a mom, consider building a more hopeful spirit in your daily life.

To ponder:

> Show me your ways, O LORD,
>   teach me your paths;
> guide me in your truth and teach me,
>   for you are God my Savior,
>   and my hope is in you all day long. (Psalm 25:4-5)

If a person is unfair to your children, you don't like it. And you shouldn't be unfair to yourself. You don't deserve that kind of thinking. Sweetness and love shine from moms, even on the worst days, and with these things comes meaningful and powerful living.

As a mom, have hope. Ask for God's guidance along the way.

Maybe you have long been a believer in Christ and have grown up in the church, you study the Bible, and you pray steadily. Perhaps you are uncertain, feel unworthy in your faith, and struggle to utter even a brief word of prayer. Or you are a mom who doesn't consider herself much of a churchgoer or who feels she knows little about God's love.

Most moms put themselves into categories—remember the box I slipped into as a child? When it comes to having faith and being hopeful, it is easy to put yourself in a box and not know how to get out. Many moms judge themselves against other women, believing other moms have the spiritual component worked out and know how to trust and hope. A mother might even believe she and her family are being punished because of bad moves she made.

Think of yourself as an upset son or daughter. If your child is unhappy or hurting or fearful, you try to calm, reassure, and remind him or her of your love. God wants to do that in your life—and that can build hope in you as a mother.

The love of God and the grace of Christ Jesus are crucial to your overall life and to your joy as a mother and the influence you will have on your family. I rely frequently on this scripture, quoted here from *THE MESSAGE* version of the Bible:

> So here's what I want you to do, God helping you: Take your everyday, ordinary life—your sleeping, eating, going-to-work, and walking-around life—and place it before God as an offering. Embracing what God does for you is the best thing you can do for him. Don't become so well-adjusted to your culture that you fit into it without even thinking. Instead, fix your attention on God. You'll be changed from the inside out. Readily recognize what he wants from you, and quickly respond to it. Unlike the culture around you, always dragging you down to its level of immaturity, God brings the best out of you, develops well-formed maturity in you. (Romans 12:1-2)

To have true hope, to make it past the rough spots and get up and start over as the need arises, you need the love and grace of God. This is not a formula that works only for those who can locate any scripture or always seem to know the right thing to say, who are at church regularly and whose children have great manners and make good grades. It works for all.

An "Inside" Job

That, of course, is what the world sees, what is on the outside. Don't be led astray by the world around you, a world that sees hurry as a necessity and worry as a staple. To be hopeful as a mom and to develop a relationship with Jesus Christ, consider the astounding you, the person you are on the inside. No one is perfect, and you will get certain things right and make mistakes along the way.

"We all make mistakes often," says James 3:2 (CEB). **God's love for you is so great that you are forgiven, even when you stumble, especially when you stumble.**

For many years I worked in a newsroom, and staff members were experts at getting the best results from their computers. If they couldn't find a built-in way to accomplish a task, they would come up with a workaround. I see that same skill in moms— queens of the workaround.

They figure out how to solve problems and to make things happen, even when it isn't automatic. This is what hope looks like on some days, the ability to work around the roadblocks and speed bumps, to get where you need to be despite detours.

A friend has a beautiful deck—built around a big tree. Just like that, you do what you need to do in life. You figure out solutions.

Living with hope helps give up fear. Fear comes easily, whispering in a mom's ear in the middle of the night or when she drops her child off at school. It can eat at you, making it hard to have hope. As you work on solutions, you begin to worry less. You expect things to go right. You know you're smart enough and strong enough to get through times when things go wrong.

A friend for many years and the mother of four children mentions a favorite passage on her journey to be hopeful: "We also rejoice in our sufferings, because we know that suffering produces perseverance; perseverance, character; and character, hope. And hope does not disappoint us, because God has poured out his love into our hearts by the Holy Spirit, whom he has given us" (Romans 5:3-5).

As this mom says about the passage: "The full life Christ promises isn't necessarily one in which we have the best-behaved children, nicest things, cleanest home, and strifeless marriage. I've found when I yield my life to Christ and his plans, when I'm willing to sacrifice, suffer, and persevere, that my hope has grown. I'm blessed with the intangibles: love and fellowship with my husband and children, and a deep satisfaction in a job 'well done.'"

Becoming a Believer

If you have questions about growing as a believer or becoming a follower of Christ, talk with your pastor. If you are not a member of a church, ask a trusted friend or coworker to recommend someone to guide you. Throughout the journey of motherhood, you will need wise counsel. On the subject of faith, much momentum can come with help from a person God sends your way to help you learn. Seek out such people, people of hope and faith.

The world changes quickly around us, and that makes the foundation of God in a mom's life even more critical. When you are concerned about what will happen as your children grow older, as they face the challenges of a world that can at times be cruel and unkind, remember to trust your steady God.

Hopeful reminders from Bible verses:

"Jesus Christ is the same yesterday, today, and forever!" Hebrews 13:8 (CEB).

"Every good and perfect gift is from above, coming down from the Father of the heavenly lights, who does not change like shifting shadows" (James 1:17).

"Don't be afraid; just keep trusting," Christ told a synagogue leader in Mark 5:36 (CEB).

"Be happy in your hope, stand your ground when you're in trouble, and devote yourselves to prayer" (Romans 12:12 CEB).

"Those who enter into Christ's being-here-for-us no longer have to live under a continuous, low-lying black cloud. A new power is in operation. The Spirit of life in Christ, like a strong wind, has magnificently cleared the air" (Romans 8:1-2 THE MESSAGE).

Take a step out in trust—with hope. Just as you watch your children grow, changing before your very eyes, you will see your faith mature.

At our little cabin at the lake, there is a row of red footprints on the window frames, the tiny feet of babies in our family who have grown so quickly. While we lament how fast time goes, we rejoice as the children flourish, becoming strong individuals whose feet will take them through the world, where they will leave special marks. So it can be with your faith. Watch it grow.

Know that sometimes it will seem harder, sometimes easier, to live with hope:

- **Learn as you go.** You may take a few steps forward and then slip back a few. Keep trying, and you will continue to grow as a mom. Remember that you don't have to be perfect, but that giving it your best can make you a more hopeful woman.

- **Make a list of your talents, your strengths, the memorable mom moments you've had.** Don't focus on what needs fixing until you learn to celebrate what is going well.
- **Make God part of this.** Being a mom is a fantastic job with huge rewards—but it is also a challenging role. Having God's help, praying, watching your prayers be answered, and coming to know more about the Bible can help you build hope as a mother.
- **Pay attention.** Adjust your mind-set and attitude as needed.
- **Realize what a tremendous positive effect this can have on your own life, the lives of your children, and the lives of others around you—this hope that comes, ultimately, only from faith in God.**

Hurry and worry erode a hopeful heart. The more you hurry, the tireder you get. The tireder you get, the more you worry. The more you worry, the less hopeful you are. And so the spiral goes.

Get Rid of Murphy's Law

Many people expect things to go wrong. They wait for the other shoe to drop. They live under Murphy's Law—"Whatever can go wrong, will go wrong." I even wrote a book called *Goodbye, Murphy's Law: Whatever Can Go Wrong, God Can Make Right.* I'm convinced that hopeful living can change the world, starting with one person. Why believe always that the worst will happen? Why not hope for the best and deal with bad things when they occur?

You know that things go wrong in life from time to time. You've no doubt lived through tragedies and traumas—and more than a few downright awful days with your children. You have managed to come through the bad times with God's love and mercy.

You also have had many joys and good things happen to you and around you and because of you. That, I've come to know, is the essence of hope, and it runs deep through the grace of God. We can expect things to turn out well. We can know that when they do not, God will guide. "Jesus stood up and shouted, / 'All who are thirsty should come to me! / All who believe in me should drink! / As the scriptures said concerning me, / *Rivers of living water will flow out from within him'* " (John 7:37-38 CEB).

Most moms are, by virtue of the job, control freaks. Go ahead and admit it. They so badly want their children to do well and to be safe and happy. Mothers constantly teach, guide, mold, occasionally scold, and do everything they can to make things go right. But they know that it won't always turn out that way. A bad grade will hit or a class will be skipped. Their child will snarl at them and hurt their feelings. Or a disaster will brew. Or their child will try to crawl under the altar during the children's sermon. Yes, this really happened.

Hope will help see you through. This is not empty hope, promises built on sand. It is hope that comes from learning and growing, praying and trusting, even when it is tough. "Then my soul will rejoice in the LORD / and delight in his salvation," says Psalm 35:9.

Most people do not wake up every morning with a smile on their faces and extra energy just waiting to be used. They may be optimistic, but they know the realities of daily life. But you can learn to be hopeful. You will find hope to be a tremendous resource to give you the strength and focus to do all that is required of you on a given day.

Look for steps you can take in your life.

Ask basic questions:

- What does hope look like in my daily life?
- What will I need to do to live more hopefully?
- How can I be more positive in my comments?
- Do I look for the good in each situation? How might I change my outlook?

From a mom: "I walk away from stressful things in life. If I commit to something, but it doesn't pan out, I let myself out of it. If we are somewhere and conflict arises (such as a bad patron at the movies, a rude person at the store), I remove us. I don't watch violent TV shows or movies about killing. It upsets me and causes me to worry about nothing."

Remember:

> We can say with confidence,
> "The Lord is my helper;
>   I will not be afraid.
> What can anyone do to me?" (Hebrews 13:6 NRSV)

A few suggestions:

- **Start small.** Catch your breath. It may be easy to feel worn out and somewhat letdown from time to time. That does not breed hopefulness. Take a nap. Read a good book. Go for a walk.
- **Give thanks for your life.** Even in the worst times, you have something to be thankful for. You may overlook good things ahead if you do not acknowledge past blessings. A pattern of negative thinking makes achieving your mom goals more difficult.
- **Look for the good in every situation.** Being hopeful is valuable as you teach your children how to look at the world. The world is full of "glass is half-empty" people and a fair number of "glass is completely empty" people. Raise children who look at the glass as half full or maybe children whose cups runneth over. This can have staggering results in your daily life and the lives of your family members.

EVEN IN THE WORST TIMES, YOU HAVE SOMETHING TO BE THANKFUL FOR. YOU MAY OVERLOOK GOOD THINGS AHEAD IF YOU DO NOT ACKNOWLEDGE PAST BLESSINGS.

"If I approach things with a negative attitude, then normally that's the kind of experience it will be," says one mother. "So, why not approach things joyfully? I know that might not apply to certain things. . . . It's hard to approach that root canal joyfully, but there are a lot of seemingly mundane things that, with the right approach, can be totally different experiences. Even folding laundry can be fun, if you approach it right."

A scripture often mentioned by moms deals with this:

> For surely I know the plans I have for you, says the LORD, plans for your welfare and not for harm, to give you a future with hope. Then when you call upon me and come and pray to me, I will hear you. When you search for me, you will find me; if you seek me with all your heart, I will let you find me, says the LORD, and I will restore your fortunes. (Jeremiah 29:11-14 NRSV)

In 1 Corinthians 13, often called the "love" chapter of the Bible, hope makes the top-three list of things that last, that are important. Faith, hope, and love abide. These three bind together to help moms stay grounded. Take one mom's suggestion and put your name in this passage as you read it.

Moms have scads of reasons to be hopeful. They are given the opportunity to change the world through their lives and the lives of their children. They are offered huge promises of God, including one of the most powerful, found in Ephesians 3:20-21: "Glory to God, who is able to do far beyond all that we could ask or imagine by his power at work within us; glory to him in the church and in Christ Jesus for all generations, forever and ever, amen" (CEB).

There, moms, is a reminder of why you can base your life on hope and not fear. God, through power within you, can accomplish way more than you can ask or imagine.

So, how about it? What are you asking of God? What are you imagining? What spirit are you offering to your children and to the world?

Learn to push fear out of the way with hope. Even if bad things happen, you can rejoice in hope. You can make it through suffering. Be a mom happy in hope.

Mom's Quiet Corner

Busy mom's tip
"There's nothing like lunch or coffee with a trusted friend to share both the joys and the burdens of being a mom. I come away from such an encounter feeling loved, understood, and encouraged."

A mom's special scripture
"I can do everything through him who gives me strength" (Philippians 4:13).

Mom to mom
"Whenever I am in the midst of craziness—the kids are misbehaving; my mom is sick; I have a tough day at work—I always tell myself, 'This, too, shall pass.' When I'm having a particularly difficult time, I remind myself to 'let go and let God handle it,' or I tell myself, 'God never gives you more than you can handle.' "

Prayer for the journey

Dear God, I long to be a hopeful mom, to give up fear, and to trust that all will be well. Please guide me. Help me be an example of hopefulness to my family and to others around me. Thank you for your promise. Take away my fear. In the name of Christ. Amen.

CHAPTER SIX

Organization versus Procrastination

Assess, Start, Repeat

Encouraging Word: *You can organize your life to run more easily.*

Everyday Step: *Do an activity with your family*
that makes you laugh.

My advice for moms who want to hurry less and
worry less is to learn to say no. Put God in the
center of your relationships, and all will fall into place.
Your family comes first before job or anything else.
—A Mom's Thoughts

When our granddaughter was just past kindergarten, she came for a long summer visit. After a day or two, she surprised us by asking for a clock in her room.

"You can tell time?" I asked.

"Not without a clock," she said matter-of-factly.

Moms' lives are like that in so many ways. There are many aids available to make daily life easier.

Gracie needed a clock to tell time. Moms need a host of help, ranging from the love and support of others to the wisdom to make the right decisions.

Start by relaxing. Consider this calming verse from the book of Jude. I have copied this and put it in my home and office to remind me: "Relax, everything's going to be all right; rest, everything's coming together; open your hearts, love is on the way!" (Jude 2 *THE MESSAGE*).

Use tools that work for you. "I am always assessing what is working and what is not and looking for ideas and motivations to make it all run more efficiently and smoothly," says one mom.

Balanced Diet for Planning Life

A young mother of two compares balancing the demands placed on a mom's life to consuming a balanced diet. Nutrition experts recommend certain numbers of servings daily from various food groups. A plate loaded with all meats or all desserts might be tasty—but wouldn't be good for you: "In a mom's life, God could be considered the plate, serving as the foundation for all other areas. The plate itself can be divided into sections, including husband, children, work, others, and self. The goal is to strive for a balanced plate over a period of time, not necessarily daily. For example, if an entire weekend is spent with children working on a science fair project or having company over for them, it might be time to focus on your husband soon after that. If work consumes much of your time during a busy week or month, try to put that further down on the list when possible to focus on a community service project. While balance such as this can be elusive, just striving for it will have a positive result."

Never a Letup

Just as you can't tell your child to pick up his dirty socks once and never mention it again, you can't slow down one day, quit fretting so much, and then never think about it again.

"A mom longs for a sense of completion, but as a mother there is often not a lot of completion," one colleague told me.

Another says, "When I am finished with laundry, there's another load waiting for me. When I've cooked a meal, we're only a few hours away from needing to eat again."

"There's never a letup," says a mom. "That's the hardest thing. I'm a goal-oriented person, and with raising kids, nothing is ever finished. You turn around and there's a new problem."

They also recognize that the incompleteness is one of the joys of being a mom, the process of watching children grow and learn and become the people they were meant to be, even while mom strives to become the woman she was meant to be. "It's really hard to shift gears," says one mother. "But I have learned all the rest doesn't matter. I need to just put other things aside and be with them."

This is an active decision. "The key to peace in my life— whether being a mom or anything else—is that certain things in

> PUTTING THINGS OFF
> MAKES THINGS
> HARDER THAN THEY
> HAVE TO BE. IT MAKES
> THEM STAND OUT
> AND TAKE OVER
> YOUR LIFE.
> PROCRASTINATION
> DRAINS YOUR ENERGY
> AND STEALS YOUR
> PEACE.

me only God can meet," says an extremely hardworking mother of a large blended family.

Stay on Track

Your old friend, the word *no*, can help you get organized, meet deadlines, and quit putting things off. Moms and deadlines are a volatile combination when it comes to moods and fun, crankiness versus coziness.

Build in extra time to meet deadlines, so you don't get frantic if you or a child gets the flu, if your spouse has a fender bender, or if an unanticipated glitch tries to grab your day.

Have you ever tried to wipe out a stain on a shirt in public, and it keeps getting bigger? Putting things off can be like this. It makes things harder than they have to be. It makes them stand out and take over your life. Procrastination drains your energy and steals your peace.

A newspaper executive with a young daughter says, "I set priorities on importance. I take care of the immediate needs while also making preparation for long-term tasks, so I'm not up against it to deliver on time. I am so much better at saying no these days. Really, it happened once my child came along. Before, I would go out of my way to assist others. Now I prioritize the need on importance as well as on development. By development, I have to make sure I'm not hindering the growth of someone else by doing a task that they're more than capable of handling. It comes easy to say no when I know it's not crucial that it gets done or when my track record shows I have been more than accommodating in times past. In those cases, I move on with a clear conscience."

If you work outside the home, look for ways to set boundaries with your schedule. In research for earlier books, *Hurry Less, Worry Less at Work* and *Hurry Less, Worry Less for Families*, I enjoyed watching creative ways that parents handle work. You may fall into the trap of believing you have little control over your schedule. However, you can often make creative suggestions and come up with answers.

- **"Be fully engaged at your job, but don't let it zap all of your energy so you can't be fully engaged with your family when you come home,"** says a mom with a business career. "Exercise—walking or bike riding—helps in decompressing from the workday and renewing energy for home."
- **"Resist the influence of peers and their children,"** says an older mom. "Don't try to do or have everything that the other mothers or their children do or have. Making your child play soccer when he would prefer to draw or read books puts unnecessary pressure on the child and the mom."

Useful Lists

Lots of moms use to-do lists to help keep them on track. Before you run from the idea of a page full of things you should do, consider how a list can lighten the load on your brain.

One mom works on her schedule like this: "I try to have a list of things I need to do each day and prioritize it by what needs to get done with what will make me fulfilled. If I only did what needed doing, I could be governed by the urgent instead of me dictating my day. I call it purposeful living."

She continues: "I learned how to make two lists when life was stressful—a right-now list that has some things I can accomplish quickly and, therefore, cross off right away and feel like I was accomplishing something, and a list of projects that would take more time to work on. This always seems to help me relax my mind and focus on getting goals accomplished."

From another mom: "I focus on what *must* be done and what *must* be done *now*."

This is an excellent reminder that everything on your list is not evenly weighted. One item will take little time and energy. Another will be more daunting.

- **Spend a few minutes studying your to-do list.** What could you get done in an hour? Set aside an hour, run through the list, and do those things. I can almost guarantee you this trick will make you more organized and help you feel calmer. Make sure your lists are in sync with your priorities. Instead of letting a list evolve into a two-ton weight about to wipe you out, use it to guide you and ease brain strain. Strike off items that don't match What's Most Important.

- **Keep lists realistic.** To remind you again: you can't do everything. No way. No how. Make decisions about What's Most Important, at work and at home and in your volunteer efforts and other activities.
- **Come up with a list-keeping system that works for you.** This is your designer list, customized for you and your family. Some people like to make one at the start of the day. Other moms make one at night for the next day.
- **Use the sticky note, one of the great inventions of our time.** Moms have so much on their minds that it's hard for an idea to take root. In other words, they forget.

Put a sticky note on the back door to remind you to take that birthday gift to your coworker or to go to your dental appointment at 3:00 p.m. Or, put the note on your bathroom mirror.

- **Update your calendar from your to-do list.** That way you won't plan a family outing on the night of your small group party at church or make a dental appointment the day you have your office potluck.
- **Put goals on paper.** Set your own deadlines. Don't try to do everything at once, but get going. Daily decisions shape big accomplishments. I compare this to cooking a meal. Everything doesn't go into the oven at the same time. Plan separate steps for projects in your life at home or work, and watch your priorities come together.

- **Don't panic.** If you feel as though you can't possibly get everything done, take a deep breath, and make hard decisions about what needs to go. Perhaps you'll get to those another time—or maybe you never really needed to do them anyway.
- **Let your children be part of the solution.**

From a mom: "At an early age, start teaching the children responsibility. Have them put their plate in the sink when they're done eating. Have them make their bed and clean up their toys. It's less work for you, and it's teaching them to take care of their things."

- **Look for little things that give big relief.** This can even be having time to clean your house or asking your spouse or another trusted person to take care of your children while you go to the grocery store. "My husband knows that a clean house is what energizes me, so he will take all the kids out so that I can clean by myself," says the mom in a large family.

A stay-at-home mother says, "I have friends whose houses are magazine perfect all the time. I have noticed that they spend most of their time cleaning, and yet very rarely is anyone ever at their house. My house is a mess most of the time. People are in and out constantly. If they judge me, they judge me."

- **Understand your family.** "I try to focus on meeting each of my children's unique physical, spiritual, and emotional needs in a mindful, consistent way. This is another challenging category," says a friend. "Because I have four children, we spend a lot of time all together, and naturally I spend a lot of time with the baby. Therefore, I try to spend one-on-one time with each of the older children as often as I can. Again, this does not have to be excessive in length or expensive. This one-on-one time does not have to always involve major chunks of a day. It can be small chunks of time here and there."

Modern families deal with many different situations, such as parents who work away in the military or other jobs. To handle that effectively, fall back on your priorities.

"Keeping your routine as routine as possible helps," says a mom whose husband has been routinely deployed overseas. "I ensured the boys talked to him as often as possible and shared their days with him and made plans with him for when he was coming home. . . . When my husband was in Iraq, I made sure I had one-on-one time with both boys and that we talked about where he was and what he was doing."

From a mom: "If your house isn't clean, it can wait until another day. Their clothes don't have to be perfect. Enjoy your children and their hiccups along the way. They will soon be grown, and you'll miss it."

Being a mom means there are many logistics to manage, and outlining the specifics makes things easier. As another mom explains: "Keep contact and important information readily available—doctors, family members, friends, babysitters, day cares, schools, coaches, bus drivers, auto club, and so on. Have an emergency game plan, and make sure all the players know their roles. If schools close at 11:00 a.m. because a water main burst and you're in a critical meeting, who can/will pick up your child and where will he go? If you're at the mall and your child falls down the escalator, who needs to be notified to meet the ambulance at the hospital? Do you have all your insurance information?"

Such organizational steps can cut down on worry. You know where things are, so you don't frantically search desk drawers, countertops, and closets for what you need.

This is a reminder, too, for getting the information you need to make decisions that are based on wisdom and not worry. If you are concerned that your child is not growing quickly enough or is developmentally delayed, see a professional and get the information you need. Your child may be all right, and your worries are for naught. If this does need attention, you'll have the facts to proceed.

The same goes with schoolwork. Moms lose sleep over how their children are doing at school, whether they'll make good enough grades to get into the middle school they want, whether they have the skills to make it to the college of their choice. Look at how your children are doing. Talk with teachers. Work with your children on their homework. Help them—and quit worrying.

As you get organized, consider the role of technology in your life—particularly in your home. Decide how much access to computers your children will have. Come up with ways to monitor their use, to make certain that they are not being preyed upon online or that they are not going to inappropriate sites.

Just do your best. And, rely on these words: "Above all else, guard your heart, / for it is the wellspring of life" (Proverbs 4:23).

When you begin to waver, get disorganized, and feel out of control, pause and reflect. More guidance from Proverbs can help: "Let your eyes look directly forward, and your gaze be straight before you. / Keep straight the path of your feet, and all your ways will be sure" (Proverbs 4:25-26 NRSV). These simple words offer a simple prescription. Keep in mind what is before you. Don't be drawn off course.

Mom's Quiet Corner

Busy mom's tip
"Being available is of utmost importance. Those open arms mean as much to an adult child in crisis as they do to a small child with a scraped knee."

A mom's special scripture
"Whatever you do, work at it with all your heart, as working for the Lord, not for men" (Colossians 3:23).

Mom to mom
"You just have to sit back sometimes and breathe. Take stock of all the blessings around you. Especially with children, those blessings are everywhere."

Prayer for the journey

Dear God, you tell me yes in so many ways in my life. You give me so many opportunities and possibilities . . . and you always remind me of what is most important. Give me wisdom to say no when needed, especially when I overschedule. I need this help in ways I cannot express, but you know my heart. Forgive me for overloading. In the holy name of Christ. Amen.

CHAPTER SEVEN

Making Choices, Facing Changes

Realigning Your Life When Needed

Encouraging Word: *You can make wise decisions.*

Everyday Step: *Pause before you make up your mind.*

> *I was burned out and bitter with everyone. I knew*
> *I needed a change, and I started praying fervently for one.*
> *For about two years, I continued to pray for a change.*
> *And you know what happens when you pray for*
> *a change? You get one.*
> —A Mom's Thoughts

Several years ago a friend gave us a cutting from a flowering bush, passing along an heirloom plant that had put on quite a show in her yard and in her parents' yard. We promptly put the sprout in the ground, choosing a spot where everyone could watch its explosion of growth and color as the months passed. Only it never flourished. In fact, it barely clung to life.

My husband wanted to mow over it, tired of its being in the way. I wanted to coddle it, certain one day it would reach its potential.

Another year passed. An inch of weak growth occurred. One pitiful pink bloom showed itself.

Frustrated, my husband dug it up and planted something else in the spot. Since I couldn't bear to kill it outright, we stuck it in a black plastic pot on the side of our garage, consigning it to death from benign neglect.

But the bush loved that spot. It grew several feet in one year and bloomed profusely. It slipped its roots out of the pot and into the ground, choosing its permanent home.

This plant offers an oft-needed lesson for moms. Change could be needed. That change may require hard choices. You will sometimes find yourself wondering whether you're in the right spot for you and your family. Since you can't do everything, you must identify what is most important and make choices accordingly.

Many moms have told me about the pain of uprooting themselves, often because of commitment to their children. Much thought, prayer, and soul-searching goes into such decisions. Rely on your priorities as you consider changes. Doing your best, you can figure out what is most important in your life and what God wants you to do. Sure, there will be times when this is like trying to read an eye chart without your glasses. It can seem blurry and ill defined. But it's not a contest that you are set up to lose. It's an adventure that moms are challenged to enjoy.

When the Big Decision Looms

"The biggest decision I have made since the birth of my child is to change my career path," a mom says. She describes her career as a journalist and the satisfaction she got from it. "However, once my daughter was born, I realized that being a mother was now the most important thing I would do for the rest of my life. Being a journalist became what I did, not who I was. I enjoyed working at the paper and I loved the people I worked with, but it was taking time away from my family—more than I wanted it to."

She prayed and, with feedback from friends and family, decided to become a teacher. "I know this is the path God has placed me on, and I am in awe of all the blessings I have received from him throughout this life change."

From a mom: "We have moved four times in our twenty-five years of marriage. Each time I learn something new about myself, and God seems to take us some place where I am going to grow in a particular area."

The mother of four sons, ages nine through sixteen, said she has not worked outside the home since her first son was born: "I am constantly faced with people 'judging' that choice. I have learned for the most part to ignore other people's perceptions and/or my assumptions about what those perceptions are."

When you are making tough choices and facing changes, seek insight and wisdom. The most direct words about wisdom:

> But anyone who needs wisdom should ask God, whose
> very nature is to give to everyone without a second thought,

without keeping score. Wisdom will certainly be given to those who ask. Whoever asks shouldn't hesitate. They should ask in faith, without doubting. Whoever doubts is like the surf of the sea, tossed and turned by the wind. (James 1:5-6 CEB)

Making tough choices can often cause you to second-guess yourself and be double-minded. These verses remind us that when we do so, we toss and turn. Be specific about your dreams, and make a plan to help them come true.

Details, Details, Details

You will be called on to make many decisions each day. You may remember the moments when you made big decisions through life—college or career, where you would live, the person who would become the father of your children. Maybe you thought you could make big decisions and rock along after that, with life falling into place along the way.

As moms grow, they realize life is a constant series of decisions, of so many varieties it is hard to imagine. Situations can range in a matter of moments from deciding whether a movie is appropriate for a middle-schooler to whether a child can wear *that* outfit in public to whose turn it is to choose a television show to watch to what vegetable the family is most likely to complain least about at supper.

And those are only the small details.

Life brings along others, such as what, if any, job to take, whether to relocate and make the children change schools, or how to care for an older parent.

Packed schedules sweep moms along and push them into doing things they really don't want to do. They are too rushed to stop and consider, or too tired to argue, or so worried as to be unsure about what matters in a given situation.

A key step: don't consistently make decisions that go against your priorities. At times you'll find yourself with a project at work or a commitment at church or a school matter that pulls you in different directions. That is to be expected. But if this happens day in and day out, step back and assess what you're doing and why.

Decide to Decide

Good decision making is a skill—one you can learn and one you can teach your children. Some decisions require lots of waiting and praying. Others are clear from the beginning.

- **Break big matters into bite-size pieces.** Don't try to change everything at once.
- **Do research and get information to help you make the right decisions, whether it is to take a new job or to let your son or daughter play soccer.**
- **Sleep on a decision when possible.** Give yourself time to consider.
- **Make the best choice you can at the time for those decisions that must be made on the go.** Don't lament. Give it your best at the moment.

- **Ask for feedback from those you trust**—your family, close friends, a pastor, or a colleague.
- **Determine the milestones you hope to reach with your family.** What steps do you need to take to move toward them? Consider the pace of life that best suits you. This is often an indicator of changes that need addressing. Perhaps you are a high-energy person who enjoys being on the go. Maybe you like to nest and spend more time at home.
- **Accept changes you weren't prepared for, and deal with them as they occur.** Surprises pop up. I think of a friend who was divorced for years before remarrying. She had a teenager—and then came the much-anticipated newborn daughter. Then came the surprise—the baby boy! Their household is full of noise and play and lots of love.

When one mom's husband was sent overseas, she had two young sons, adopted and having transition challenges. She said, "This required more time than I could give while working full-time, so I stopped working full-time. Some people don't have that option. Some would say we didn't either, but our priority was our sons, not maintaining a certain lifestyle. . . . It's difficult for me personally not to be a wage earner, but what I am able to provide my family by being at home right now is immeasurable."

- **Don't be paralyzed by past mistakes.** Reflecting on the past is not about regrets, roads not taken, or bad decisions. It is about considering what worked—and what you might need to do differently. Learn from the past. Acknowledge events that you had little or no control over, and ponder how you reacted. How we respond to unplanned—and even unwelcome—events can make the difference between being content or frustrated.

- **Don't compare yourself to others, a tendency that many moms mention.** This is especially true when you are making hard choices. Everyone won't agree with you—and many people will have opinions. Your decisions will be based on what is right for you and your family, based on prayer and the counsel of people you trust and your priorities for your family.

"Everyone has advice, even people without kids. Just smile and say, 'Thank you,'" says a mom with two young children.

Moms often assess their "performance" as mothers, find themselves lacking, open the door, and usher in guilt by the truckload. They think other mothers do it better, get it right. They feel as though they don't do anything as well as

REFLECTING ON THE PAST IS NOT ABOUT REGRETS, ROADS NOT TAKEN, OR BAD DECISIONS. IT IS ABOUT CONSIDERING WHAT WORKED—AND WHAT YOU MIGHT NEED TO DO DIFFERENTLY.

they should. Perhaps you have done that a time or two when you faced a choice or a change.

Preparing for Change

Although some changes are unpredictable, others you will see coming. One of these is how your household differs depending on the age of your child. Don't dread the teen years, but know you'll have different challenges than you had with a toddler. If you have a young child, know your time and energy will be used differently. Says a brand-new mom, "I never realized how much free time I had before! But I think the thing that has surprised me the most is that I've adjusted. And other new moms will too."

As children mature, not only will you be forced to make a host of choices, but you will want to teach them to make good choices.

"As our children grow into adults," says a mom who gets a tear in her eye when she speaks of her firstborn going to college, "we have to be able to give them room to be themselves while gently prodding them in the direction of the choices that we would have them make. Allowing them that space opens up avenues of communication that would not be there if you simply dictated their choices. I feel that my sixteen-year-old communicates with me pretty well. We talk about different ways that different people handle situations and what the results and ramifications are of their choices. My hope is that this openness will continue through adulthood, and our relationship will be better because of it."

"The key is to embrace each season, and that is easier said than done," says one mom of young children and also older children who have moved out of the house. "When the kids were all young, I used to think about what it would be like when they were older. Now that they are older, I reminisce about the 'good old days.' When they were young, it was a physical exhaustion that threatened to overwhelm me. Now that they are older, it is more of a mental exhaustion that I fight."

Another mom emphasizes the importance of communicating as children get older—and if they get into trouble. "I wasn't prepared to see my adorable, precious boy" turn into an angry teen, she says. So she regrouped. "How did we get from there to here?" she asked. "What do I have to do?" That led her to a fierce commitment to keep communicating, wanting to know she had done all she could. "Really keep the lines of communication open no matter how horrible the relationship is. Then you see glimmers of hope."

From a mom: "All relationships, even those with your children, must be developed, and I suggest being intentional about it. Yes, this even applies to your children. Obviously when a child is born, you have certain responsibilities that dictate how the relationship develops. However, the older your children get, if you don't adjust the way you treat them to their current age and interests, then that relationship can't develop to its fullest."

Do you need to make changes in how you are treating your older children? Are you intentional in your relationships with your family, or have you gotten into a rut?

Moms face so many choices, and many are often good. That's where it gets tough. It's a little bit like those designer boxes of chocolate candy that appear at Valentine's Day. You know that any piece you choose will be good, but it's tough to know which one.

Live easily within your choices. Figure out the process that works for you. Then make that your rhythm and your routine.

When I was a child, I loved to play the game of Pick Up Sticks, where you dumped the little colored sticks out and tried to move one without disturbing the others. Life can be like that. It's tough to do. You'll have unintended consequences. You'll upset the other sticks.

Rely on these promises:

- **"It is God who arms me with strength / and makes my way perfect" (Psalm 18:32).**
- **"He will keep you strong to the end. . . . God, who has called you into fellowship with his Son Jesus Christ our Lord, is faithful" (1 Corinthians 1:8-9).**
- **Be mindful of how fast time goes.** "I know it's a cliché, but as you age, you realize you've spent too much time focusing on what won't last," says the mother of four young adult children. "If I could go back and do things over, I'd not change my decision to be a stay-at-home mom with my young children. But I'd be much more in the moment with my kids—not worrying about the next meal, scheduled event, or whether or not my kids had everything

materially. When my kids are gone, it's the conversations and laughter I miss. This must have been the most important all along; we're just too busy when we're young moms to realize it."

- **Don't be afraid of changes or choices.** "Our Lord Jesus Christ himself and God our Father loved us and through grace gave us eternal comfort and a good hope. May he encourage your hearts and give you strength in every good thing you do or say" (2 Thessalonians 2:16-17 CEB).
- **Be intentional about the changes you make.**
- **Consider the gifts God has given you.**
- **Use these words of comfort:** "Trust in the LORD with all your heart and lean not on your own understanding; / in all your ways acknowledge him, and he will make your paths straight" (Proverbs 3:5-6).

Mom's Quiet Corner

Busy mom's tip

"Assign reasonable and age-appropriate chores as early as possible. Children who learn responsibility at home do better in school because they bring an established work ethic to their studies. Additionally, many hands make light work."

A mom's special scripture

"For God did not give us a spirit of timidity, but a spirit of power, of love and of self-discipline" (2 Timothy 1:7).

Mom to mom

"I think for moms going through tough times, whatever it is, find that inner strength inside you through prayer or whatever guides you, and tackle it. Rely on family, friends, coworkers, church family, whatever it takes to get through it. Most moms have people in their lives who are more than willing to help. To me, it is a sign of strength to accept help when you need it."

Prayer for the journey

Dear faithful Lord, thank you for your steadfastness. Help me be faithful in everything I do, at home and in the world around me. Help me be a strong model of love and faith for my children. Give me wisdom, God. In your mighty name. Amen.

CHAPTER EIGHT

Prayerful, Not Fretful

Leaning on God in a Hectic World

Encouraging Word: *You can turn to
God with all your needs.*

Everyday Step: *Pray in your car as you head
to work or run an errand.*

*I have made so many "official" parenting errors.
But two things I have done consistently—
and they cover a multitude of sins or parenting blunders—
I have loved my children unconditionally
and prayed for them regularly.*
—A Mom's Thoughts

I pray."
That's how many moms get through demanding days. How they handle the challenges of daily life. How they wave bye to

CHAPTER EIGHT

Prayerful, Not Fretful

Leaning on God in a Hectic World

Encouraging Word: *You can turn to
God with all your needs.*

Everyday Step: *Pray in your car as you head
to work or run an errand.*

*I have made so many "official" parenting errors.
But two things I have done consistently—
and they cover a multitude of sins or parenting blunders—
I have loved my children unconditionally
and prayed for them regularly.*
—A Mom's Thoughts

I pray."
That's how many moms get through demanding days. How they handle the challenges of daily life. How they wave bye to

their little ones at nursery school or to their teens driving off in the family car.

One of my favorite stories is from a young working mom with a preschooler, who relies on a prayer taken from the first book of the Bible: "I wrote this verse down on a card and put it in my purse the first day I went back to work and had to take my daughter to day care. I still have it in there. 'The LORD watch between you and me, when we are absent one from the other'" (Genesis 31:49 NRSV). Or as the verse reads in another version (NIV): "May the LORD keep watch between you and me when we are away from each other." Or from *THE MESSAGE*: "GOD keep watch between you and me when we are out of each other's sight."

What a powerful prayer for all moms!

Moms pray to start the day and saturate the atmosphere of the home. They pray to help a child through a painful divorce or a grandchild through a problem at school. They offer prayers for safety, for healing, for wisdom, for good grades or the right position on the community team.

Consider how this mom stays focused with three children, ages thirteen, eleven, and nine: "The single best thing I do to

"I RE-CENTER MYSELF ON GOD EVERY MORNING. I SIT IN MY KITCHEN, AND IT'S QUIET . . . JUST ME AND GOD, AND GOD NEVER FAILS TO MEET ME."

walk with God is to take time for our relationship first. It means I sacrifice a little sleep to wake up before everyone. . . . I adore my husband and my children, but in everything I do, I try to put God first. It is amazing how much I don't miss that hour I give to God. In fact, it makes the day go more smoothly because I re-center myself on God every morning. I sit in my kitchen, and it's quiet— no children, no husband, no dog, no cooking—just me and God, and God never fails to meet me."

A Spiritual Foundation

One part of the mom journey is building a spiritual foundation, growing in closeness to God. Many moms quickly acknowledge that it is God's grace that carries them through their days.

Do not be disappointed in yourself or feel unworthy. Take small steps if needed to learn to pray, to ask for and accept God's forgiveness. You have the ultimate trainer for your role as mom.

This reminder from 2 Corinthians 3:5: *"Our competence comes from God."*

Set aside a few minutes for meditation. Add a minute or two as you can, building a time of prayer into your life. Let this become a necessity for growing as a mom, not a luxury. Even in the noisy worlds of moms, guidance will come through.

As you begin to step back to review your life in a quiet time, you may find that you are again holding yourself to an unrealistic standard. Or maybe you haven't slowed down long enough to notice when things go right. The world around you may define *success* in one way, but perhaps success looks totally different to you.

Remember these words from Psalm 131:2: "I have stilled and quieted my soul." Training yourself to still your soul, you can be more equipped to say no as needed and to be ready when God brings new opportunities into your life. "This is why it's necessary for us to pay more attention to what we have heard, or else we may drift away from it" (Hebrews 2:1 CEB).

As Doors Open

God opens more doors than you can imagine. Often those bring questions and details to be worked out. To find peace, set aside time for solitude. You may want to take a walk and pray.

Times of reflection can be unsettling. You may feel restless, guilty, and even nervous. Your mind may wander, and all those things you feel that you *should* be doing will pop into your mind. Whisper the prayer of "help" to God. Find a verse of scripture that you can read again and again to bring you back to a calmer place.

How does a busy mom build a prayer life? "A little bit at a time," says one prayerful mom. "It may start out as thirty minutes in the morning. Then you pray throughout the day, at the red light, waiting in line at the grocery store, washing the dishes, folding the clothes. Whispers of prayers throughout the day add up. Also the biggest motivation for praying for your children is the realization that no one will pray for your children with the fervency or love that you possess."

An executive with a young daughter says, "In the mornings and evenings I take time to pray. But the truth is, I pull on God for strength whenever I feel I need to throughout the day."

One grandmother and mother says having a prayer partner helped her greatly: "As mothers, we're programmed to respond to others. We'll do for others what we don't do for ourselves. I found I would get up because I knew I was accountable to my prayer partner and vice versa. She called when I overslept and had made up my mind not to get up. And I did the same for her. After praying together, I then would spend more time alone—just me and the Lord. Why is this important to you? Without time alone with the Lord, you lack the power that is needed to set the atmosphere in your home that guides your family into God's loving presence that day."

This is helpful for a working mom whose husband has been sent overseas more than once, a mom who, besides working and parenting, regularly ministers to others in need. "Every time our family is going through a change or a major choice is coming up, I fast and pray. I believe Scripture tells us to do this," she says. She joins with a group of others to do so. "It makes us more invested in each other's lives and makes us more aware of prayer needs."

From a mom: "God comes first. Instead of trying to find time to squeeze prayer into my schedule, my schedule is fitted around prayer. For me, it is best to rise before the household, offer my whole day to Jesus in prayer, read Scripture, and collect myself while I drink my coffee. When I fail to do this, I cannot even begin to tell you how different my day is . . . and it is not for the better. I also pray throughout the day. In fact, I try to make my whole day a prayer."

This prayer time helps you stay in tune with what matters. "Keep your focus on the best. Be still and listen to the Holy Spirit," says the mother of four young adults. "Don't let others set your goals or standards." As one way to do this, she recommends watching less television and paying less attention to advertising.

Use Your Gifts

Look back on your time as a mom. Reflect on the path you have taken, and think about how you have grown. Use reflection time to learn more about your gifts and talents. Knowing your gifts from God can help you serve your family and the world around you with more energy and enthusiasm.

Your gifts may very well be quite different from your neighbor's, your best friend's, or anyone else's, as the Bible outlines for you: "Now there are varieties of gifts, but the same Spirit; and there are varieties of services, but the same Lord; and there are varieties of activities, but it is the same God who activates all of them in everyone" (1 Corinthians 12:4-6 NRSV).

Spending time in prayer, listening for God's direction, can help you understand your gifts and see holy assignments for each day. Knowing what your gifts are helps you understand your children more clearly. Just as you are unique, so are your children. You begin to observe your children's gifts and encourage them to develop their strengths.

The Power of Questions during Prayer Time

At first your quiet time may help address the way you spend your time and energy in a hectic world and how you want to shape your family, the lessons you want to teach your children, the big things that need addressing and the little things that need tossing. Moms are good at asking questions and figuring out answers. Asking the right questions in your life and pondering the best answers can be effective during your prayer time.

Here are basic ways to get started with a prayer journal:

- **Write questions in the journal and pray about the answers.** If you are not consistent with this, don't let that stop you. Do it when you can. As the power of this time takes root, it very well may become a valued habit.
- **Consider your goals, dreams, and priorities.** What's most important to you?
- **Assess your daily actions, how you use your time and energy.**
- **Take steps to make sure that the way you use your time and energy lines up with your priorities.** If you want one thing and do another, you will seldom feel at ease.
- **Think about what you like about your life as a mom and what you want or need to change.**
- **Ponder what is going to have to happen to make those changes.**
- **List the things that fulfill you as a mom.** List your blessings. Say thanks.

From a mom: "Our senior pastor did a talk on journaling through Scripture. It really hit me head-on. I had been trying on my own to read more deeply, but it never occurred to me to keep a journal, to pray for revelation before reading, to stop when I heard God's whisper and start writing right there. . . . I went home from the retreat, and I began the next day. That was seven years ago, and it has really grown from there."

Try this: read a psalm each morning.

At a meeting for writers, I shared a room with a colleague. Each morning she read a psalm aloud to start our day. This simple act, prayer from Scripture, set the tone for the day and reassured me as I walked into the world.

The Psalms are full of prayerful reminders that can give a mom courage and wisdom for the day. Consider these examples:

- "Answer me when I call to you, / O my righteous God. / Give me relief from my distress; / be merciful to me and hear my prayer" (Psalm 4:1).
- "In you, O LORD, I seek refuge" (Psalm 31:1 NRSV).
- "Have mercy on me, O God, / according to your steadfast love; / according to your abundant mercy / blot out my transgressions" (Psalm 51:1 NRSV).
- "Praise is due to you, O God, in Zion; / and to you shall vows be performed, / O you who answer prayer!" (Psalm 65:1-2 NRSV).
- "We give thanks to you, O God; / we give thanks; your name is near. / People tell of your wondrous deeds" (Psalm 75:1 NRSV).

The Bible is clear on the power and importance of prayer: "If any of you are suffering, they should pray. If any of you are happy, they should sing" (James 5:13 CEB). Pray. Pray. Pray. The Bible describes this as powerful and effective. This is a practice that can blossom with study, a willingness to ask God for forgiveness, faith, quiet, and space for yourself.

Prayer can seem hard. Perhaps you haven't prayed for a long time. Or you never quite understood how to pray. Maybe you feel as though God is far away and not listening. Consider these words in Romans 8:26-28:

> Meanwhile, the moment we get tired in the waiting, God's Spirit is right alongside helping us along. If we don't know how or what to pray, it doesn't matter. He does our praying in and for us, making prayer out of our wordless sighs, our aching groans. He knows us far better than we know ourselves. . . . That's why we can be so sure that every detail in our lives of love for God is worked into something good. (*THE MESSAGE*)

Here's a simple verse that is a good companion as you sit alone: "His name is the LORD— / be exultant before him" (Psalm 68:4 NRSV). *Exultant* is such a strong, happy word—and it speaks to your time with God and your time as a mom. Take a deep breath and center yourself. Remind yourself that this is about becoming the mom and the woman you were created to be . . . you, special, creative, unique.

Start each day afresh, with the possibility of joy and the commitment to less juggling. This is a new day with a clean slate. It arrives with the promise that God's mercies are new every day. Recall Lamentations 3:21-24:

This I call to mind,
    and therefore I have hope:
The steadfast love of the LORD never ceases,
    his mercies never come to an end;
they are new every morning;
    great is your faithfulness.
"The LORD is my portion," says my soul,
    "therefore I will hope in him." (NRSV)

Reflect on each of these words as you cultivate joy. Read through the following, and see if a phrase speaks especially to you during your quiet time:

A new day.

God's great faithfulness.

Morning by morning.

New mercies for you, Mom, every single day.

Wait for God's salvation.

Wait.

"But I'm not that good at waiting."

Wait anyway.

Appreciate this new day.

This day promises to make your life more fulfilling: God's faithfulness. God's mercy.

Soak it up.

Savor it.

A new day.

Write a phrase or two from those verses on a sticky note or a piece of paper, and keep them handy. Refer to them, as the day unfolds, to help you stay focused on holding onto the freshness of the moment.

"Keep on praying and guard your prayers with thanksgiving" (Colossians 4:2 CEB).

Mom's Quiet Corner

Busy mom's tip
"Don't overplan. Then you get in a bad mood. The children are happier when I'm not trying to plan things for them because then I spend time with them, and I'm not frantic."

A mom's special scripture
The LORD your God is with you,
    he is mighty to save.
He will take great delight in you,
    he will quiet you with his love,
    he will rejoice over you with singing. (Zephaniah 3:17)

Mom to mom
"Prayer is the ultimate solace and a source of comfort. When I am most distressed, feeling helpless, I can still offer prayer for my child and for myself as her parent. The comfort of knowing that God is as close as 'Father, help me' is beyond expressing—it is indeed peace beyond understanding."

Prayer for the journey
Dear faithful God, thank you for hearing my prayers. Remind me to turn to you often each day, to seek your guidance, and to follow your prompting. I pray for my children, that you will watch over them and keep them close to you. I pray for my abilities as a mother, that I will be loving and wise and raise them well. In the sweet name of Christ. Amen.

CHAPTER NINE

When Your Battery Runs Down

Rested, Renewed, and Refreshed

Encouraging Word: *More rest can help you have more energy.*

Everyday Step: *Plan a special treat just for you.*

> *Sometimes I feel extremely overwhelmed. To recharge*
> *and renew, I like to sing, paint, take a nap, read,*
> *pray, make myself stay home and rest. . . . I always*
> *think better and get more done if I take time to rest.*
> —A Mom's Thoughts

My husband built a bird feeder, a tripod made out of big stalks of Louisiana bamboo. He hung a dish in the middle. Immediately a squirrel started trying to figure out how to gobble up all the birdseed. Watching him reminded me that if you set your mind to something, you can usually do it. The squirrel slowly learned to shinny up the bamboo, although that took practice. Then he stretched his skinny little body as far as he could and tried to get a paw on the container. Then he slipped and fell the three feet to the ground. So he got up and did it again. And again. Until within minutes he had figured out how to scramble from the edge of the bamboo onto the container, keeping his balance while it swung wildly. Slowly the platter, now emptied of half its seed, would steady, and the squirrel would eat away.

Does this in any way remind you of how you approach life? Is it possible you've gripped the spot where you are standing, stretching as far as you can, and then taken a tumble? But do you get up and try again—and eventually work it out?

Moms often are not so good when it comes to finding time for rest and relaxation, the time that renews, the time that feels like putting on a comfortable pair of slippers after a day of wearing high heels. Set your mind and heart to it, and make it happen.

Many children have one of those inexpensive little toys that you wind up and then let it go. Often a child will play with this on a tabletop, and one of three things happens. The toy winds down and stops abruptly, it falls off the edge of the table, or the child grabs it. Have you had that feeling lately in your life?

Time to Recharge

Moms need time to renew—even if it is only a few minutes of quiet time in the morning or a soak in the tub in the evening.

Sounds simple, doesn't it? But the Mom Thing kicks in, and it's hard to sit down. There's one more basket of clothes to fold, the mad dash for a clean school uniform, or the dishwasher that needs unloading—so it can be loaded again. So many mothers tell me they feel guilty when they take time for themselves.

But taking *care* of mom is a crucial part of *being* a mom. That's even a commandment in the Bible: "All the Law has been fulfilled in a single statement: *Love your neighbor as yourself*" (Galatians 5:14 CEB). This verse carries a potent reminder—you are to love others as yourself. That means you must love yourself.

From a mom: "I need to ensure that I care for my basic physical needs before I can be of help to anyone. By this, I mean getting the proper amount of sleep and exercise that I know I need to function at my best, eating and drinking healthily, and time. Sometimes I'm so busy I forget to eat or I can go all day without a drink of water. And considering and caring for my own mental and emotional health. . . . I'm talking about meeting my basic needs in a balanced, proactive, healthy, and consistent way so that I can be the best caregiver I can be."

"This is probably the hardest thing," says one mother. "I take a hot bath when I can . . . not long, but luxurious. A mani-pedi is a nice splurge. I usually go for the cheap kind, but it makes me feel pretty and pampered."

"Ahhh! A hot bath does wonders," says the mom of four, including an infant. "Sometimes I just rest, take a nap. Sometimes I sit in quiet . . . when I can find it. I love to read spiritual readings or take a run around the block. My prayer time is both my rest and recharge. I suffer when I don't have it."

A mother with an infant, her first child, says, "When you've had enough, take some time. Period. One weekend I did this by sleeping every chance I got. I left my husband to do pretty much all of the feeding and changing of the baby. It was such an unusual move that he was concerned. 'Are you having a breakdown?' he wanted to know. No, I wasn't having a breakdown. I was just taking some time. My husband survived, and so did the baby. And after I did that, I felt a lot more refreshed."

Take time to do things you enjoy each and every day, little and big. For many this is having fun with the family, setting aside quiet time, reading, working in the yard, or taking a walk around the neighborhood. Many women have hobbies such as scrapbooking, knitting, or photography. Exercise is vital to many moms, activities that range from jogging to bowling to tennis to bicycling.

From a mom: "I take a few minutes to be completely selfish with my time. I love to read. It is an absolutely wonderful thing to sit and read a book without interruptions. After putting the kids to bed and readying the house for the next day, I put off any 'unnecessary chores' and read."

"I love getting together with my friends," says another mom. "I have a wonderful group of girlfriends from my Sunday school. Twelve of us get together once a month to play Bunco. I meet with three of those women every Wednesday night for prayer and accountability." But she also recharges alone: "Reading a book for fun is a great way for me to relax. I also enjoy sewing—something I am really trying to get better at."

A mom with children from preschool to college says she recharges by spending time with her husband, time that is not always easy to find. She enjoys a fun treat, such as going out to eat. She's one of many moms who enjoy a girls' trip, and she recommends spiritual conferences with a group of church women. "They give you hope and a refocus on your priorities." Bring out the best in each other. Help each other.

Self-care can make you into a new and better person.

- **Get enough rest, which can be hard when you need to stay up late to take care of chores or work in a few moments for yourself or get up early to get the household going.** You may have to do less reading (gulp) or give up a favorite TV show to get to bed earlier.
- **Take care of your health.** Get regular checkups. Don't let worrisome physical issues go untended.
- **Don't take on too many volunteer jobs.** And don't take on too few. As you know, serving others is fulfilling and can be renewing. But when you overload, you may find you give so much to others that you have little left for yourself or your family.
- **Get a room in a bed-and-breakfast in a nearby town if you need alone time.** Take a good book, favorite music, and your journal. Enjoy being pampered with someone else cooking for you. A little bit of time away can help you come home energized and engaged.
- **Schedule a getaway weekend alone or with a friend or your spouse.** It doesn't have to be a big, expensive trip. Plan

activities you enjoy, such as a day of antiquing or a bicycle ride or maybe a hike on nearby trails.

- **Make time for your mate.**

From a mom: "Schedule alone time for yourself and adult time for you and your partner. It sends a message to your kids that you are just as important as they are and parenting is not just about being a chauffeur or handmaiden. If you respect yourself enough to take advantage of personal time and space, your kids will reflect that in their interactions with you, and that makes life easier."

- **Look with new eyes at ways to have fun.** The logistics of daily life overshadow fun that may be right before your very eyes. Try different things. Maybe you used to enjoy going to movies but have gotten out of the habit of going. Maybe you would relish a walk in the park, letting someone else keep an eye on the children.
- **Make the most of weekends or whatever days you have off if you work outside the home.** "I try to cut back on commitments during the week, focusing on work, family, and resting. Then on the weekends, I put work on the shelf," says a mother. "Even though many of the weekends are spent simply 'reloading' for the next week—buying groceries, doing laundry, cleaning—we try to carve a block of time, usually Friday night, to see a movie or do something special . . . no cooking, no chores. It makes going back to work on Monday much easier when you feel like you've done something interesting during the weekend."

- **Allow time for spiritual renewal.** Perhaps this is a quiet day alone, a women's retreat, or a class at church. Maybe it is starting with ten minutes of prayer and Bible reading in the morning, building a habit of daily renewal.

From a mom: "For spiritual renewal, attending Sunday school and church provides a weekly boost of encouragement. Reading a daily devotional, even if only for five minutes, helps keep the pressures of parenting in perspective. Praying throughout the day reminds me that I am not alone in this job of being a mom."

- **Ask for help from your spouse or someone you can depend on.** Says a busy mother: "I find support in staying connected with God, but my mom is a rock, my husband always encourages me to do more than I ever dreamed, and my prayer/accountability group (three moms) as well as my Bible study (has met once a month since our oldest kids started elementary school eight years ago) are places I turn when I feel beaten down."

"If you can let your mate know what you need and how he can help you so you can function at your best, that is the key," says another mother.

- **Exercise.** Oh, my, this is difficult for many moms, but it can be a major stress reliever and help you stay healthier. Regular exercise reduces stress, can help you lose weight, and gives you energy. Plus, you may be renewed by being outdoors during the process. (I find exercise to help in many ways, but remember to check with your physician before embarking on a strenuous exercise plan.)

"When I am active, my frustration level with children, husband, work, and life is much more manageable," says a part-time teacher with three children. "I enjoy walking a few days a week with a friend. The visiting is another great release. In addition, when I know that she will be waiting for me alone outside my house if I don't get up, I get my bottom moving. The camaraderie and friendship with the folks at my swim team are also great. I don't know them as well, but it is a positive, encouraging environment."

From a mom: "I suggest exercise to work off some of the energy generated by anger; this has seemed to help. It raises the level of endorphins, lifting the mood, and is physically beneficial in relieving stress."

If you have not exercised in a while, do not try to become an elite athlete overnight. Get checked out by your doctor, and start slow. But don't hesitate to start.

Headed for church recently, I was stopped by a train. Written in large letters on the side of one of the rail cars were these words: "Home shop for repair. Do not load train." This same approach can benefit moms. Identify times you need to go in for "repair," to get rest and relaxation. Don't load your schedule up during these times.

How do you get everything done?

You don't. You don't even try. Instead, you get the most important things done first, step by step. Enjoy that process.

"Don't be so hard on yourself," a grandmother and mother of a grown daughter says. "No one can live up to her expectations of herself, and God never condemns you. Allow Christ to live his life through you. Rest in him, knowing that he beckons moms who are weary and heavy-laden to enter this rest. Take up his yoke, for his yoke is *easy* and his burdens are *light*."

Here is that fantastic reminder in Scripture: "Come to me, all you who are struggling hard and carrying heavy loads, and I will give you rest. Put on my yoke, and learn from me. I'm gentle and humble. And you will find rest for yourselves. My yoke is easy to bear, and my burden is light" (Matthew 11:28-30 CEB).

Needed news: the phrase "learn from me" jumps out in this passage. "Learn from me." Look at the life of Christ. He loved so completely. He taught. He healed. He visited with friends. And he always made time to get away and pray. Using his model for your life as a mom is a good way to renew and quit second-guessing yourself.

Grab again this reassurance: "And you will find rest for yourselves." Be patient with yourself. Part of your growth will be to understand your own timing, the pacing of your life and flow of activities you prefer. This may be at the core of how you live your life with your children.

In the same way that your children grow and learn, you will mature as a mom. Listen for God's guidance, especially in those mom moments when you are weary and need a boost. Choose how you will spend your time and energy. Act on what you learn as you grow as a mom.

God promises. God delivers. Believe that God will do what God says.

> When life is heavy and hard to take,
>   go off by yourself. Enter the silence.
> Bow in prayer. Don't ask questions:
>   Wait for hope to appear.
> Don't run from trouble. Take it full-face.
>   The "worst" is never the worst.
> (Lamentations 3:28-30 *THE MESSAGE*)

Enjoy Friends

Says one mom of three: "If moms don't find a group of friends to support each other, I'm not sure how any mom can stay sane. When I get together with one of my groups of friends, we can let go of all the frustrations. When I'm having a difficult time raising a teenager, I have people to pat me on the back and pray for me to help me take one more step."

Another mom agrees: "My biggest outlet is being with other women, doing good deeds, and stealing time for myself. Being with people who are in relatively the same or similar boat helps. I can tell when I need a break because I get very cranky and frustrated with life." Her commitments include serving as president of a professional women's group and selling cosmetics for fun: "I really enjoy pampering and supporting women and helping make them feel better about themselves." She also gets together with a group of friends "monthly to have food, drink, and good conversation."

From a mom: "I take time to pour into myself with hair appointments, massages, and simple indulgences. I have to refuel on all levels so I can pour out into my family and others. If I'm on empty, I have nothing to give to anyone else."

One mother longs for one night a week to herself, "time off, a night where there's no guilt with it." This time for moms could be to sit in the bedroom and read a book or go out with a friend.

You may not need much time away.

"I HAVE TO REFUEL ON ALL LEVELS SO I CAN POUR OUT INTO MY FAMILY AND OTHERS. IF I'M ON EMPTY, I HAVE NOTHING TO GIVE TO ANYONE ELSE."

Perhaps a night a week. Perhaps less. One thing I notice is that moms are eager to have the house to themselves or a little time away. But then they start feeling lonesome, missing the family or being overwhelmed by the quiet—recharged, they are ready to get back with their families.

Take your inspiration from Christ, who always had people pressing in around him and was in demand with giving sermons and healing and doing God's will. "Early in the morning, well before sunrise, Jesus rose and went to a deserted place where he could be alone in prayer." (Mark 1:35 CEB). The second part of this passage sounds like something a mom could hear: "Simon and those with him tracked him down. When they found him, they told him, 'Everyone's looking for you!'" (Mark 1:36-37

CEB). Christ had taken time out and was ready to move on, to go to nearby villages. Retreating and renewing can prepare you to move more strongly back into the family fray.

Mom's Quiet Corner

Busy mom's tip
"Cut yourself some slack. We put a lot of pressure on ourselves to do everything 'right.' But, you know, sometimes there can be more than one right way. You don't have to follow all the books, advice, or guides exactly so."

A mom's special scripture
"This is the day the LORD has made; let us rejoice and be glad in it" (Psalm 118:24).

Mom to mom
"Ultimately my level of happiness and peace is a result of where my relationship with God is."

Prayer for the journey
Dear God, I offer you praise for the many blessings you heap upon me. I ask forgiveness for overlooking the goodness of each day. Help me express gratitude to you in the way I live each day with my children. Through the holy name of Jesus. Amen.

CHAPTER TEN

What Matters Most

Powerfully and Memorably Mom

Encouraging Word: *As a mom, you are changing the world.*

Everyday Step: *Focus on what matters most to you.*

*We have the power to push through each day. That's how
I'm living, even when it's tough. I say, "God, you
woke me up so I need you to give me the strength to
press and push through the day." And each night I realize
he did! It's a wonderful feeling to know he's got my back.*
—*A Mom's Thoughts*

Perhaps you or your child has played the board game Chutes
and Ladders. Sometimes you move up the ladders.
Sometimes you slide down the chutes. Being a mom can feel just
like that. You feel as though you are right back where you started
on the journey of Momhood, still too rushed, too fretful. Don't be

afraid to start anew. You aren't going in circles, even if it seems like it. Take stock of what you need. Consider this list:

Wisdom	Humor
Energy	Kindness
Patience	Insight
Love	Focus

One mom, a teacher with two small children, leans on Matthew 28:20: "And, lo, I am with you alway" (KJV). She says, "Every single day I wear a bracelet with this inscribed on it. It is a constant reminder that God is always walking beside me."

Make the Ordinary Extraordinary

The weight of being "a good mom" can be heavy at times. You may be concerned that you are not making the kind of progress you want or that your children are not flourishing. Through these nagging worries, remember that fun can make all the difference.

- **Enjoy more time for fun as a family.** This will shape your children in surprising ways—and have terrific impact. To so many moms it is the key to remembering what having a family is all about. Even though you have a host of heavy topics to deal with, having fun can change your attitude, give you energy, and bind you together as a family.

A friend from church says her memories of playful times as a child guide her to be more playful with her children: "The good things I remember often include 'play' times. I remember playing house with my cousin—which doll was going to be mine, what was my baby's name, and which movie star would I marry? I remember the playfulness that occurred day in and day out at my grandparents' house. At their house there was fun associated with most things, from grocery shopping to cooking to watching TV to raking leaves. Maybe that's why I strive for more things to be playful than not. I don't want the ordinary to fall through the cracks, so I try to make as much as I can a little 'out of the ordinary.' I find myself thinking that we only get to do this once, and I want to do it right. I want my children to remember a lot, and I want it to be for the right reasons."

- **Celebrate.** Make special occasions special. Make everyday events special. Is it the shortest day of the year and the day for hot chocolate, cupcakes, and a game? Is it a holiday? Add an extra touch, something that brings a smile to your face and the faces of your children.

It seems as though hurried and worried moms forget how to have fun. Everything is a chore or a duty or something that needs to be checked off a list. When you remember, you will be amazed at how it feels.

- **Play with your children.** Be silly or do the unexpected. Doing this can add energy to your life as a mom and reinforce your family life on the hard days.

"Parenting is almost always fun for me," says a young mom. "Seeing in my daughter's eyes that I am the most important person to her is the most fun." Remember that you are special, you are important, and you fill a special place in a child's heart.

Consider these words from the mother of four: "The best way for mothers to have a playful heart is to follow their children's lead. I often pray for God to give me a heart as happy, as playful, as loving, as forgiving, as resilient, as patient, and as beautiful as the hearts I see in my children. It is no wonder that Jesus calls us to be like the little children in order to enter the kingdom of heaven."

She adds these delightful words: "If you need a more playful heart, study a three-year-old closely. I often say everyone needs a three-year-old somewhere in his or her life."

- **Take a vacation.** "I *love* vacation!" says a mom. "It is the best time to just be a family. It doesn't have to be a grand tour—although that's nice—just a weekend or a night or even a day away from the world we live in. In the summer, we plan an outing for one day of every week, and it's just us together. I've been blessed with some really neat little individuals who are really fun to be with when we're not focused on the training and rearing. Those are the days when God and I have the best time together as well, so I guess it still comes back to the fact that my relationship with my kids should mirror God's relationship with me."
- **Include other families in activities.** "We have been intentional about cultivating friendships with families who have

children the same age as our children who enjoy the same things," says the mother of two daughters and a son. "We vacation together; we go out to eat together; we sit together in church. By doing these things together, we not only have great friends, but the kids are entertained, and it's so much better than just being with their siblings all of the time. We are developing great memories with family and friends."

- **Don't make activities difficult or complicated.** "To enjoy time with my children, it most often does not involve anything too complicated," says a mother. "They are happy just playing a round of Go Fish—or any board game of their choosing, dancing silly in the kitchen, cuddling up to read a story. At times the best thing you can do is to stop what you are doing to play whatever it is they are playing. Because of my children's wide age span, this can range from Mr. Potato Head to LEGOs to painting toenails turquoise to a computer game."
- **Be exhiliarated through this spirit of playfulness and with the essence of life as a joyful mom.** In Proverbs 31, the Bible outlines the characteristics of a woman of strength. Verse 28 states, "Her children rise up and call her happy" (NRSV). Let this be part of the legacy you leave your children.

One of my favorite questions to ask women is who has had the greatest influence on their lives. Most times the answer is their mother or grandmother. The role of mom is powerful and meaningful. Seeds that were planted years ago may yield a harvest in years to come. Sometimes miraculous results sprout on the spot.

- **Think about what you want to pass along to your family.**
  "My mother is an optimist. We are similar in that regard,"
  says the mother of three. "But she is so opposite of me in
  that she is very organized and quite a perfectionist. I am a
  perfectionist at some things, but I don't sweat the small
  stuff. My mom and her mom are very close—two women
  with unshakable faith and devotion to their God, their
  spouses, and family. I learned from them that if God is the
  center of any relationship, it can work. I learned from them
  that you should love your spouse and that love should
  reflect the love of Christ."

Most people have a favorite season. If you ask, they're quick to
say spring because everything is fresh and new, or autumn because
the trees are so beautiful, or winter because it brings Christmas,
or summer because of vacation and time in the sun.

Ask a mom what her favorite part of being a mom is, and she'll
tell you—spending quiet, precious moments with a child, playing
a game, watching a son or daughter blossom.

**What is *your* favorite part of being a mom? *Always* include
time in your life for those moments, whatever they are.**

**Turn your life and the lives of your family members over to
God, knowing that you are doing incredibly special work here
on earth.**

Rely on these powerful words: "I'm convinced that nothing
can separate us from God's love in Christ Jesus our Lord: not
death or life, not angels or rulers, not present things or future
things, not powers or height or depth, or any other thing that is

created" (Romans 8:38-39 CEB). "My favorite verse of all time," says a mom. "Nothing can separate me from the love of God! How awesome is that."

Make no mistake: you are changing the world through your family.

> ## WHAT IS *YOUR* FAVORITE PART OF BEING A MOM? *ALWAYS* INCLUDE TIME IN YOUR LIFE FOR THOSE MOMENTS, WHATEVER THEY ARE.

In 1 Corinthians, Paul spoke of the ministry of the apostles of Christ. Could this be your ministry as a mom: "Think of us in this way, as servants of Christ and stewards of God's mysteries. Moreover, it is required of stewards that they be found trustworthy" (4:1-2 NRSV).

As I was writing this book, a dear friend died, the mother of childhood friends who have been close to me for years. Her funeral was a celebration of her life and what she stood for, her faith in God and her love of music.

At her service, a family member said, "Her lifelong desire was to share Jesus with children. She tried to brighten the day of everyone she came in contact with." Even when she was older, losing her eyesight and becoming frail, she encouraged me as a writer. Her children brought her to my first book signings, and she always greeted me with a smile and a hug.

While her family mourned, their tears were mixed with smiles.

She was a giant of a woman who influenced everyone whose life she touched, starting with her family. When her husband suffered from dementia, he often could not remember her. One day a nurse asked him, "Do you know who this is?" He looked at his wife, puzzled, unable to call her name, and then said, "Love." She was love in all that she did, and she wanted nothing more than to share the love of Christ with those around her.

Her children explained the things she taught them, a list that ranges from "unconditional love, without regard to race, social status, or income level, respect for others, humor, the skills and love of music, and that the Bible has the answer to all of life's questions."

In the Sermon on the Mount, Christ outlined the role of believers, and these words speak volumes to the importance of faithful moms: "You are the salt of the earth. But if salt loses its saltiness, how will it become salty again? . . . You are the light of the world. A city on top of a hill can't be hidden" (Matthew 5:13-14 CEB). Your life can add flavor to the world, a brightness that would be diminished without your influence.

On the map of your life, you have made it this far. You are here.

Now is the time for you to be salt and light.

Most parents have had a few times—at least—when their children talked back to them or tried to get in the last word. Your brain will likely try that same trick as you move forward on this journey, especially when you come to forks in the road.

That little voice in your head may very well tell you that a more joyful, playful, prayerful, faithful, peaceful lifestyle as a mom won't work for you, that other women can slow down and enjoy each day more but not you. Or the voice may tell you that you tried this before and it didn't last. Or that you're in too deep or don't have the support you need.

Before long those doubts sound like a lecture, a parent scolding a child. You begin to tell yourself all the things you're doing wrong, the long to-do list you need to get to before the week is over and, for good measure, the list of mistakes you've made in the past.

Stop.

You don't have to be perfect—nor should you expect that of yourself. God doesn't. You can't do everything, but you can do what matters most.

Again: you will need to stop and get your bearings along the way. Turn to Jeremiah 6:16:

> Thus says the LORD:
> Stand at the crossroads, and look,
>   and ask for the ancient paths,
> where the good way lies; and walk in it,
>   and find rest for your souls. (NRSV)

Most moms wish they could find the good way and stay on the path. But life has its detours and potholes and roadblocks. The fantastic thing is that God guides, wherever the road goes, if you pause and listen. That direction comes in many ways—from the words of dear friends and family, including small children, from sermons and songs and the Bible and all sorts of other books.

As you move forward as a mom, don't forget to ask from time to time: "What's next, Lord?

"What's next for me to use my gifts and serve my world and my family?

"What's next to model a less hurried and less worried life for my children?

"What's next to live fully?

"And how?"

Take heart as you move forward. This great work that has been started in you will be seen through to the finish line. Write this verse where you will see it when you think you aren't going in the right direction: "I am confident of this, that the one who began a good work among you will bring it to completion by the day of Jesus Christ" (Philippians 1:6 NRSV).

"What's next, Lord?"

Go forth with the peace of God. Hold these words from Jude 24-25 close to your heart: "To the one who is able to protect you from falling, / and to present you blameless and rejoicing before his glorious presence, / to the only God our savior, through Jesus Christ our Lord, / belong glory, majesty, power, and authority, / before all time, now and forever. Amen" (CEB).

Mom's Quiet Corner

Busy mom's tip

"I find that if you don't take yourself so seriously, life is a lot more fun."

A mom's special scripture

Blessed are those who trust in the LORD,
> whose trust is the LORD.

They shall be like a tree planted by water,
    sending out its roots by the stream.
It shall not fear when heat comes,
    and its leaves shall stay green;
in the year of drought it is not anxious,
    and it does not cease to bear fruit. (Jeremiah 17:7-8 NRSV)

Mom to mom

"While there are many challenges to being a mom, it is also extremely rewarding and meaningful. To truly enjoy time with my children, I intentionally remind myself how short the time is that I will have with them in the scheme of things. . . . Reminding myself of this helps me focus on enjoying being with them now."

Prayer for the journey

Dear God, thank you for my family and this ministry you have given me as a mom. I ask for your ongoing guidance in making me the mom you want me to be. Please help me hurry less and worry less. Please use me to make this world a better place, to serve you. In your holy and breathtaking name. Amen.

DISCUSSION GUIDE

My advice to other moms would be to cherish every moment
they get to spend with their children.
—A Mom's Thoughts

H*urry Less, Worry Less for Moms* can be used for individual
reflection or as a group study, including as a discussion
guide for a Moms Group. The study tools revolve around prayer,
reflection, and Scripture.

Using this book's ten chapters as an outline, the guide provides
for each chapter:

- A key point for moms to consider
- A reflection on a favorite Bible passage recommended by a
  mom
- Discussion questions
- A step for each mom to take on her journey

This study weaves biblical teaching into everyday life and can
help moms find ways that God's words affect daily actions for

mothers. The Bible is an ancient parenting guide, filled with fresh truths for today's families, a book filled with useful and vibrant suggestions for life today.

Moms may find it hard to incorporate renewal time into daily life, and this study guide can help start a habit of prayer and reflection. In addition, groups of moms can use the questions for discussion.

This study invites participation, but it also focuses on individual journeys, recognizing that each family is different. It is suited for moms of all ages and in various situations of life. Moms find themselves in unique places as parents. This means that responses to the questions are personal—and differ greatly.

This study can also help develop a community of moms who share the challenges and blessings in the adventure of being a parent. It is suitable for a small group, a women's vacation Bible school or Sunday school class, or a Hurry Less, Worry Less Moms Group.

Tips for Individual Study

Moms find personal study time helpful—and hard to make a habit. This book can help you carve out time for quiet reflection or make your prayer time more meaningful. No matter how busy you are, do not feel as though you are stuck in quicksand. Keep looking for ways to tackle the challenges of being a mom, juggling many different activities, and to enjoy the blessings that come with your family. As you listen for the voice of God, you may encounter many blessings and learn how to do a variety of new things in your role as a mom.

Developing or refining the habit of prayer, reflection, and Bible study can help you grow spiritually—and help you approach your role as a mom in a more joyful and peaceful manner. Each chapter of this book is filled with questions for you to ponder and can provide fodder for your individual study. As I interviewed moms for this book, they said that answering questions helped them review priorities and consider needed changes. Perhaps you will also find that to be true.

Questions and key points in this guide can direct your quiet time, as you are led. Consider using a journal or notebook to write your ideas and to think about how God might speak to you each day.

A journal can help you sort out your thoughts in a noisy household, write prayers, or set goals. If you aren't ready to keep a journal, jot notes in the margins or inside the covers of this book (unless you borrowed this copy from someone!). I mark books in pencil, making notes on what speaks to me—an item I want to remember, the date, an "aha" idea, an inspirational quote, or a reference to a scripture I want to think about more. I have found that writing things down almost always clarifies my thoughts and helps me understand the best next steps for my life.

Do not let a lack of time for study bring guilt or disappointment. Look for a few moments here and there until you discover a rhythm that works for you. As you seek quiet time, you will find that it is well worth it and can pay off with peace, joy, and hope, attributes that give you extra energy for each day.

One approach is to read a chapter and consider what it says to you. Ask God to give you wisdom and discernment, to use the book to help you grow. I have written this book in sections, with many at-a-glance lists so that a mom can dip into it as she has time, whether sitting in the car waiting to pick up a child from school or in the lunchroom at work.

Many mothers contributed to this book, and visiting with them reminded me of the influence that moms have on the world. My prayer is that this study guide will lead the way to an ongoing prayer and study time in your life. You may falter, but if you do, try again. Just as you care about the details of your children's lives, God cares about your life and has a plan for you.

Start a Hurry Less, Worry Less Moms Group

One of the excited suggestions of a mom who contributed to this book was to gather a group of mom friends to socialize and study the book, a way to stay on track, have renewal time, and build a community of stronger, more energetic mothers.

- How this can work: invite a few friends to join you on your journey. Almost every mom struggles with too much to do and too little time, so you should have little trouble finding folks who need such a discussion.
- Perhaps you can make this a celebratory gathering of friends, with refreshments and conversation to go along with the study of the book. Maybe it can be an evening meeting for renewal or relaxation.
- Ask members what meeting time works best for them, whether they want daytime or evenings, whether they want

to meet weekly or less frequently, for an hour or two or three. Moms can read a chapter in advance and jot down thoughts at home, then come together to discuss their observations.

Moms not only *want* to talk about these issues; they *need* to talk about them. Inspiration—and determination to live more fully as a mom—can come from one another.

Take This Journey with a Friend

Perhaps you do not want to add a meeting or study group to your schedule. One possibility is to enjoy this journey with one mom friend, perhaps someone you want to see more often but haven't found time for. Commit to read the book together and discuss it. You might choose to have an e-mail discussion with an out of-town-friend (or sister or sister-in-law or other relative) where you chat briefly about issues you face and how you are moving forward. Or plan a daily walk and discuss it as you exercise. Moms are wonderful encouragers to other moms, and such a study can be a personal setting in which moms become closer and learn from each other.

Use This as a Small Group or Women's Sunday School Class Study

A small group or class at church can help you connect with other moms who deal with issues similar to those in your life.

Perhaps you are already a member of a small group and looking for a study that will speak to a group of diverse moms. Maybe you have felt called to start a group and have noticed a handful of other moms in your congregation who might need a place where they can go deeper in their faith. Or maybe you've wanted to teach a women's vacation Bible school class while your children are in their groups.

- Remember: you do not have to be a preacher or a Bible scholar to lead a small group. You simply have to help pull the group together, encourage others, and depend on the Holy Spirit. If you feel called to lead a group, prepare for each class, read the material in advance, and jot down an agenda.
- Notify members where you will meet and when. Trust that God will guide each member. This class is focused on helping other moms learn to live more fully, nourished by God's guidance and grace.

Reminders for Group Leaders

Moms may regard this class study as a time of conversation and fun, as well as study, or they may be on a tight schedule and want to stick to the book. Get feedback from the group and use your own intuition as to how long the classes should last. While you do not want to rush through the material, keep an eye on the clock. Do not cut speakers off, but keep the discussion on track. Remember, some participants have chosen this class because they are too busy, so time is probably an issue.

This book can be used as a ten-week study with one chapter for each week, or as a six-week study, starting with an introductory discussion and covering two chapters in each of the following weeks.

It can also work for a vacation Bible school class in a variety of formats. One suggested approach is four nights, covering the introduction and the first two chapters on night one; chapters 3 through 5 on night two; chapters 6 through 8 on night three; and chapters 9 and 10 on night four.

Encourage participants to read the chapters in advance and to consider how God might be speaking to them. Ask them to pray for the class and for what they might learn or offer to others. When moms come together to talk about God's guidance, each woman brings something different and wonderful to the group.

If possible, make your meeting space more personal and comfortable. You might add a candle or a cross or an item that is symbolic of the week's discussion. Perhaps someone in your group may want to help with this, but be careful of adding yet another to-do to a mom's schedule.

Be available to greet people when they arrive, and remember that some are shy and even uncomfortable when they first join a group. Helping moms feel comfortable is a precious way to show the love of Christ.

Many groups provide refreshments because they like to eat and visit. You might ask people to volunteer to bring snacks or a light meal. One small group that I led developed a casual system for contributing refreshments and came up with fun meals for each session.

Open each session with prayer, asking for God's presence in the discussion. Allow moms to share in the conversation, but avoid making it seem as though someone has to speak. Remind your group that discussions are confidential. Provide pen and paper for taking notes as needed.

A Sample Session

- Open with prayer and casual conversation, and provide time for chatting as participants settle in.
- Direct participants to "Growing as a Mom" below, using this as an outline for the class. Seek comments or questions on discussion from previous meetings, and check in about how the week is going. A mom may have a care or joy she wishes to share upfront.
- As the meeting begins, focus on the scripture for each chapter, a verse offered as a favorite by an everyday mom. You may also want to ask moms to volunteer to bring favorite passages for each meeting.
- Begin your discussion with "For Mom to Consider."
- Lead the group in reading and discussing the reflection/discussion questions.
- In each chapter, ask group members to choose a step they will take, and invite them to reflect on their thoughts during the course of the study.
- Assign chapters to be read before the next meeting.
- Consider asking for prayer requests as you wrap up, and pray for God's guidance for each mom.

Growing as a Mom: Reflection/Discussion Questions for Groups or Individuals

After reading each chapter, turn to "Reflect on a Mom's Special Scripture" in the study guide. Then, turn to "For Mom to Consider," and think about how it relates to your life. Use the "Reflection/Discussion Questions" to go a step further. One question may lead to a discussion that takes you to the next, or a particular topic will jump out at you. Let the Spirit guide you to spend time as needed with these questions and to reframe them to be most effective.

Each chapter ends with a "Next Step for Mom," an action you might take to make changes in your life. This is a step that you identify and commit to take, custom-made to help you move forward as a joyful and peaceful mom. God wants you to live fully and enjoy your role as a mom. Each person is different, so ask what God's will is for *your* family—and what steps you might take to be transformed in your faith and affect your family more positively. Pray about your answers, and let God shape your family.

Chapter 1

A Map for Mom: Being the Person You Are Meant to Be

For Mom to Consider: *Your family is unique, and a fresh look can help you be the mom you want to be.*

Reflect on a Mom's Special Scripture: *"Commit to the LORD whatever you do, / and your plans will succeed"* (Proverbs 16:3).

Reflection/Discussion Questions:

1. Chapter 1 mentions how easy it is to get into a "box" as a mom. Have you experienced this with your family? In what ways? Have you had times when things worked out easily? If so, how did that affect your role as a mom?

2. Many moms are so busy that they seldom take time to assess their lives. Have you found this to be true? Do you need to take a fresh look at your life? How might this change you individually and your family overall?

3. How might you benefit from hurrying less and worrying less as a mom?

4. Each family is unique, and this makes each mom's decisions different. List ways your family is special and some of your best times as a mom.

5. Some mothers try to be perfect, do everything, and feel guilty if it doesn't work out. Have you ever tried for perfection? Have you dealt with guilt as a mom? What advice would you give

a mom who feels guilty? How might that advice apply to your life?

A Next Step for Mom: *Choose a word to focus on during the next few days in your role as a mom. Keep that word in mind as you make daily decisions.*

Chapter 2

More Joy, Less Juggling: Know When to Say No

For Mom to Consider: *When you overload your schedule, you may rob yourself of joy.*

Reflect on a Mom's Special Scripture: *"Train a child in the way he should go, / and when he is old he will not turn from it"* (Proverbs 22:6).

Reflection/Discussion Questions:

1. Chapter 2 says to guard your mom time. In what ways do you do this? What are the challenges you face in doing so? Is it difficult for you to say no to activities? What tips do you have for other moms to say no when needed?

2. How does your calendar help or hurt you as you juggle activities? Are there ways you could schedule less? Are there fun activities or service projects you need to add?

3. Many precious mom moments pop up in daily life, but sometimes moms can miss them if they're too busy. List two or three sentimental moments you can recall with your children,

either recently or in the past. What might you do to appreciate such moments more fully?

4. One mother mentions her "Mommy radar" that helps her know when something isn't right with her children. Do you have a similar way to tune in to your family? What suggestions would you give another mom who wants to be aware of her child's needs?

5. Some moms disagree on quality time versus quantity time with their children. How do you feel about this? What do you do to try to spend more time with your family? Can quality moments outweigh the amount of time spent together?

A Next Step for Mom: *Take a look at your calendar, and write in a special "date" with your family within the next two weeks.*

Chapter 3

The Promise of Peace: Awareness of the Goodness of Life

For Mom to Consider: *A simple step toward peaceful living is to give thanks each day.*

Reflect on a Mom's Special Scripture: *"Humble yourselves, therefore, under God's mighty hand, that he may lift you up in due time. Cast all your anxiety on him because he cares for you"* (1 Peter 5:6-7).

Reflection/Discussion Questions:

1. In chapter 3, a mom says, "When you put God first in your life, the rest just falls into place." Have you found this to be true?

In what ways? What challenges do you face in putting God first? How does your daily life look when things fall into place?

2. Do you find it difficult to turn down the noise in your life and have quiet time? Do "peace and quiet" often go together in your life? In what ways might you build a more peaceful daily life?

3. The Bible says to "let your gentleness be known to everyone." In what ways do you consider yourself a gentle person? In what ways do you need to work on this? Do you find it easy to be drawn into "drama" with those around you? How do you avoid this?

4. One mom suggests teaching basics of safety to help cut down on possible problems. Are there areas that you need to work on with your family? What worries might be lessened by teaching certain steps to take if trouble arises?

5. Do you believe that gratitude can open the door to peace in your daily life? What are you most thankful for in your life? What makes you smile each day?

A Next Step for Mom: *Make a list of concerns that you will turn over to God for at least a month. Pray about this list.*

Chapter 4

Parenting Priorities: Blueprint for Meaningful Mom Moments

For Mom to Consider: *Keep your priorities in mind daily to live more meaningfully.*

Reflect on a Mom's Special Scripture:

Do not fear, for I have redeemed you;
I have called you by name, you are mine.
When you pass through the waters, I will be with you;
and through the rivers, they shall not overwhelm you;
when you walk through fire you shall not be burned,
and the flame shall not consume you.
For I am the LORD *your God. (Isaiah 43:1-3 NRSV)*

Reflection/Discussion Questions:

1. In chapter 4, the author tells about her mother as an example of a woman who lived by her priorities. She suggests that you figure out what is most important to you and make daily decisions that support those priorities. Do you find this strategy helpful in your life? Why or why not? What do you consider your top three priorities at this time in your life?

2. One mom mentions that she and her family define their priorities by a Scripture verse that says their household will serve the Lord. What would it mean for your household to do likewise? Are there changes you would need to make? In what ways are you now serving God as a mom?

3. Do you consider yourself a Big Picture Mom? Do you have a vision for your family life? If so, what is it? If not, is this something you might consider? Do you need help in following through on your dreams for your family? What could help?

4. In living by your priorities, you must handle distractions wisely. What draws you off course in your life? How might you solve those problems? What distractions could you eliminate?

5. Serving other people is a commandment from the Bible. But on a demanding day, doing this can seem tough. In what ways do you serve others? How might you do so? Has God been nudging you to make a difference in your community? If so, what do you need to do? Or is this a season of time when serving your family needs more of your time?

A Next Step for Mom: *Write one Mom Priority on a note card or sticky note, and put it somewhere you will see it frequently. Consider how it affects your decisions.*

Chapter 5

Building a Hopeful Heart: Expect Great Things to Unfold

For Mom to Consider: *Being a more positive person can affect your family and all those around you.*

Reflect on a Mom's Special Scripture: *"I can do everything through him who gives me strength"* (Philippians 4:13).

Reflection/Discussion Questions:

1. Chapter 5 says that moms often judge themselves harshly against others, believing they lack in trust and hope. Do you compare yourself to other mothers? In what ways could you be more positive in how you think of yourself and others?

2. "Living with hope gives up fear." In what ways do you think that statement can help in your life? Are there worries you need to replace with hope? What step might you take to do so?

3. What are some of your talents and strengths? What aspects of motherhood do you need to celebrate more fully?

4. Do you believe that most moms like to be in control and find it hard to surrender to God? If so, why? If not, why not? How might mothers learn to relax and trust God with their children and their everyday lives?

5. One mother says she makes a choice to approach things joyfully rather than negatively. In what ways do you do this in your life? In what ways might you do it?

A Next Step for Mom: *Each day in the week ahead smile and encourage someone you encounter.*

Chapter 6

Organization versus Procrastination: Assess, Start, Repeat

For Mom to Consider: *Gather the proper tools to be organized. Quit putting things off.*

Reflect on a Mom's Special Scripture: *"Whatever you do, do it from the heart for the Lord and not for people"* (Colossians 3:23 CEB).

Reflection/Discussion Questions:

1. In chapter 6, a mom says that she prepares in advance for long-term tasks to avoid deadline disasters. In what ways do you

need to change your approach to long-term projects and activities? Do you tend to procrastinate? If so, how might you do things in a more timely way? What are some suggestions you would give a friend who is stressed by deadlines?

2. Many moms use to-do lists to help keep them on track. Does this work for you? If so, how? If not, why not? What other options might you use to remember what you need to do?

3. Expecting children to help with chores is a way to stay organized at home and to help them grow. However, this can be difficult. How do you handle this? What is an assignment you need to give a child in the coming days?

4. Technology is a growing distraction and concern for some moms. Is this an issue in your household? How do you keep yourself from spending too much time on the computer? How do you monitor your family's computer use?

5. Moms may become fearful or worried because they do not have the proper information at hand. How can you gather facts as you "manage your household"? What changes do you need to make?

A Next Step for Mom: *Pick one small area in your home that needs clearing out. Get rid of the clutter, and organize the paperwork.*

Chapter 7

Making Choices, Facing Changes: Realigning Your Life When Needed

For Mom to Consider: *Life is filled with choices and changes, some planned and some unexpected.*

Reflect on a Mom's Special Scripture: *"God didn't give us a spirit that is timid but one that is powerful, loving, and self-controlled"* (2 Timothy 1:7 CEB).

Reflection/Discussion Questions:

1. In chapter 7, a mom says that she prayed two years for a change. "And you know what happens when you pray for a change? You get one," she says. Have you ever needed to make a change? How have you handled it? In what ways might this mother's statement guide you?

2. Moms frequently face tough choices about careers and must decide whether to change jobs, whether to work outside the home or be stay-at-home moms. Have you faced this decision? How have you approached it? Some moms feel judged because they have "outside" jobs, while others feel judged because they have chosen to stay at home. Do you think this is an issue in our world? How might moms deal with this?

3. Do you make choices that support your priorities? Do you find this easy or difficult? How do you shape your choices?

4. Have you ever been faced with an unexpected—and perhaps unwanted—change? How did you deal with it? What tips would you give others facing such situations?

5. Communication can be important as your family life changes. In what ways do you communicate with your children? In what ways do you handle this well, and in what ways do you need to work on this?

A Next Step for Mom: *Consider a change that you may need to make. Gather information to help you make the right choice.*

Chapter 8

Prayerful, Not Fretful: Leaning on God in a Hectic World

For Mom to Consider: *Busy moms can build a strong prayer life.* Reflect on a Mom's Special Scripture:

The LORD your God is with you,
he is mighty to save.
He will take great delight in you,
he will quiet you with his love,
he will rejoice over you with singing. (Zephaniah 3:17)

Reflection/Discussion Questions:

1. In chapter 8, many moms say they pray to help them be stronger parents. Do you ever feel that you are too busy to pray or that God is not listening? How might you build a more consistent prayer life?

2. One mother has developed a discipline of journaling as part of her prayer time. Have you tried writing your prayers or insights into Bible verses? How has this worked for you? What is another approach for those who do not want to keep a journal?

3. Do you look upon each day as a fresh start? If so, how does this help in your attitude? If not, how might you change your approach to remember that God's mercies are new each day?

4. In the book of James in the Bible, it says if you are in trouble, you should pray, and if you are happy, you should sing songs of praise. Do you find it easier to pray when you are happy or when you have problems? Do you think God listens to your needs? Do you have examples of answered prayer in your life? In what areas might you offer thanks to God?

5. Some moms have their prayer and quiet time early in the morning before their family stirs. What works best for you? What changes might you take to build a prayer time?

A Next Step for Mom: *Read a psalm one morning each week. Sit quietly and ask God to guide you in the day ahead.*

Chapter 9

When Your Battery Runs Down: Rested, Renewed, and Refreshed

For Mom to Consider: *Setting aside time for rest and renewal can make you a more energetic mom.*

Reflect on a Mom's Special Scripture: *"This is the day the LORD has made; / let us rejoice and be glad in it"* (Psalm 118:24).

Discussion Guide

Reflection/Discussion Questions:

1. In chapter 9, a mom says that she has to meet her basic physical needs before she can be of help to her family. What needs do you have in your life? How might you address them?

2. Moms sometimes find it hard to schedule simple pleasures such as taking a hot bath or reading a book. How do you recharge? What do you do to renew? What might you tell a friend about how to relax in daily life?

3. Exercise is a key part of renewal, but many moms know it is hard to make this a habit. Do you have an exercise plan? Have you had times in your life when you were more fit? Do you see a difference in your energy when you exercise and when you don't?

4. One mom longs for a night off each week, time when she does not feel guilty and can read and rest. Have you ever had a similar feeling? How do you plan time for yourself within the schedule of your family?

5. Many moms enjoy renewal through being with friends. Do you have people you connect with regularly? If so, how do they help you recharge your battery? What are some of your favorite activities to do with friends? If you do not have friends to call on, how might you begin to build such friendships?

A Next Step for Mom: *Think of one thing you would really like to do for fun, and do it within the next month.*

Chapter 10

What Matters Most: Powerfully and Memorably Mom

For Mom to Consider: *You will leave a legacy with your family. What do you want that to be?*

Reflect on a Mom's Special Scripture:

Blessed are those who trust in the LORD,
  whose trust is the LORD.
They shall be like a tree planted by water,
  sending out its roots by the stream.
 It shall not fear when heat comes,
  and its leaves shall stay green;
in the year of drought it is not anxious,
  and it does not cease to bear fruit. (Jeremiah 17:7-8 NRSV)

Reflection/Discussion Questions:

1. In chapter 10, moms emphasize the importance of having fun and enjoying time with their families. How playful are you with your children? Do you think you need to plan more fun times with them? How could you do this? If you are happy with your play times, what tips do you have for other moms?

2. One mother says it is clear why Christ instructs us to come to Christ as though children. Why is that? In what ways can we learn about life from children?

3. At times moms feel as though they are going in circles, not accomplishing much. Have you ever felt like this? What have you done lately that seemed extra special in your role as a mom? What needs a little more attention? Are you able to look at yourself as a work in progress, or do you want to check off your development one time and move on?

4. When you consider what is next in your role as a mom, what comes to mind? What excites you about opportunities as a mom?

5. What have you learned from your mother or grandmother or from moms around you? How can you use this knowledge in your daily life?

A Next Step for Mom: *Identify your favorite part of being a mom. Tell your family what you love about them.*

The following may be used as a handout and given to each group member during study meetings or as a reminder sheet for a mom. For an electronic version, e-mail judy@judychristie.com.

Ten Tips for Busy Moms
How to Stay on Course as You
Hurry Less and Worry Less

by Judy Christie
Hurry Less, Worry Less for Moms
Trust in the LORD with all your heart / and lean not on your own
understanding; / in all your ways acknowledge him, / and he will make
your paths straight (Proverbs 3:5-6).

1. Remember: you can't do everything. Focus on What's Most Important.
2. Pray and read your Bible.
3. Trim something from your schedule today. Say no to one thing to say yes to something else. Allow more room for joy.
4. Don't compare yourself to other moms. You are unique.
5. Be a positive person. Smile. Expect the best.
6. Take care of yourself. Get enough rest. Exercise. Drink water.
7. Schedule time for fun with your family. Make ordinary days special. Play with a child. Do something unexpected to make your family laugh.
8. Spend time with your mate or special friends. Get away from your daily routine from time to time. Read a book or walk around the block.
9. Give thanks for your family. List the blessings in your life.
10. Know that you are changing the world through your role as a mom.

I'd Love To Hear From You

I would love to hear about your journey and how God is at work in your life. E-mail me at judy@judychristie.com. For ongoing tips on hurrying less and worrying less as a mom, go to judy christie.com or listen to my free Hurry Less Worry Less podcast on iTunes. Remember: being a mom is a spectacular role, and you are making a difference in the world with your family. Enjoy today!